D1523946

PROSECUTING APARTHEID-ERA CRIMES?

A South African Dialogue on Justice

International Human Rights Clinic
Human Rights Program • Harvard Law School
Cambridge, Massachusetts, United States

ISBN: 978-0-9796395-1-7

Human Rights Program
Harvard Law School
1563 Massachusetts Avenue
Pound Hall 401
Cambridge, MA 02138

617-495-9362
hrp@law.harvard.edu
http://www.law.harvard.edu/programs/hrp

Distributed by Harvard University Press
http://www.hup.harvard.edu

TABLE OF CONTENTS

PREFACE

In September 2006, the Cape Town-based Institute for Justice and
Reconciliation ("IJR") invited a team of students and educators from Harvard
Law School's International Human Rights Clinic ("the Clinic") to examine
a South African government policy that had intensified questions about
prosecution of apartheid-era crimes.[1] The amended policy, quietly promulgated
in December 2005, granted the National Prosecuting Authority ("NPA") wide
discretion to decide whether or not to prosecute alleged perpetrators.

This book presents and reflects on a broad and varied collection of
South African perspectives on the enduring issue of prosecutions. The voices
are deeply personal, complicated, painfully honest, and at moments seemingly
contradictory. They embody a collective struggle to confront a past that is rife
with divisions and to negotiate a present that remains exceedingly complex more
than a decade after the end of apartheid.

During an initial trip to Johannesburg and Cape Town in October
2006, a team from the Clinic interviewed several dozen individuals, including
former staff and commissioners of the Truth and Reconciliation Commission
("TRC"), human rights lawyers, government officials, and survivors of apartheid.
In January 2007, a team conducted a follow-up trip to KwaZulu-Natal, Cape
Town, and Johannesburg for an additional two dozen interviews with individuals
including former African National Congress ("ANC") and Inkatha Freedom Party
("IFP") cadres, political leaders, and newly middle-class black families. In March
2008, a team returned to Johannesburg, Pretoria, Durban, and Cape Town to

---

[1] Prosecuting Policy and Directives Relating to Prosecution of Offences Emanating from
Conflicts of the Past and Which Were Committed on or Before 11 May 1994, promulgated
Dec. 1, 2005. *See* Appendix A. Throughout this book, the terms "amended prosecutions
policy", "amended policy", and "amended guidelines" will be used interchangeably as they
were by interviewees to refer to this policy.

conduct a handful of new interviews and to reconnect with previous interviewees to assess how opinions might have changed with the passage of time. All the narrative Reflections included in this document are drawn from interviews conducted during these trips to South Africa.

Throughout this process, we wrestled with a variety of issues. For example, although the NPA's prosecutions policy was a central concern to many interviewees, they often viewed litigation as just one piece of the immense puzzle dealing with justice in post-apartheid South Africa. As human rights practitioners, we understand the desire for accountability and prosecutions as well as the powerful role the law can play in society. An absence of prosecutions, most especially a failure to pursue high-level officials who did not receive amnesty from the TRC, raises serious questions about adherence to international rule of law standards. However, we also appreciate that other obvious needs—social, economic, political, psychological, emotional—co-exist with a desire to see perpetrators convicted for their crimes, and that these demands cannot be ignored by a society seeking to rebuild itself following prolonged division and conflict.

In the pages that follow, we attempt to capture some of the complexities and conflicting and overlapping needs felt by South Africans with diverse definitions of justice. Throughout this project, questions repeatedly surfaced concerning how best to balance macro-level challenges such as addressing social inequalities, promoting the rule of law, or ensuring economic development with deeply personal and individual issues such as lingering trauma, a desire to see a perpetrator convicted and imprisoned, or the need to learn the truth about lost loved ones. The narrative Reflections that speak to these issues are at the heart of this piece. We hope that these South African voices and perspectives will stimulate public and private dialogue and encourage a frank, ongoing discussion about the role and timing of prosecutions in transitional societies. The narratives also serve as a powerful reminder that government must listen to the concerns and aspirations of the people as it continues to shape policy, for ultimately South Africa will address the question of prosecutions through a South African process and reach a uniquely South African answer.

Tyler Giannini, Susan Farbstein, Samantha Bent & Miles Jackson
International Human Rights Clinic
Harvard Law School
Cambridge, Massachusetts
June 2009

PROLOGUE

"You should use the past as a reference, lest you forget."

John Kani, Actor, Playwright
Johannesburg, October 2006

They called us the Lookout Boys. The only requirement was that you could whistle sharp and clear. We were the guardians of activist meetings of those who came together to find ways to resist apartheid. We'd whistle when strangers came sniffing around the secret meetings so the leaders had time to disappear. From Lookout Boys, we graduated to Stone Throwers. Police cars would come, and we threw stones at them to delay the police while the meetings dispersed. Eventually, we graduated to Members of the Youth. We went to school during the day, but at night we went to another kind of school. In [daytime] school, they taught us that the white man had come to South Africa first, that we were only guests in their country. Our teachers of the night corrected the myths of the teachers of the day. In these shrouded classes, we learned we were royalty. We were descendents of kings, everyone, every family. I know it was make-believe, to instill pride and racial superiority, to empower us. We were almost arrogant, puffing our chests, feeling for the first time proud of who we were. We learned that white people were stupid, ignorant, unteachable, and that one day, they would pay.

Then in the 1960s, post-Sharpeville, things got tough. The ANC Umkhonto we Sikwe ["MK"] militia moved into townships. They began recruiting people to enlist. They were looking for soldiers, and I signed up. I must not have been a very good actor back then. My father noticed my ears

pricked up too often. He kept a tight leash on me, forbade me to join. I wanted
to be trained. I wanted to fight. I wanted to come back with an AK-47 and kill
them all. Instead, I became an actor. I went to audition for a play called *Antigone*.
During rehearsals, we discussed the right to stand up against the law if the law was
unjust. I learned it was my duty to struggle against, to expose when the law was
unrighteous. In 1972, Athol Fugard, Winston Ntshona, and I created *Sizwe Banzi
is Dead*. It was a play inspired by the feeling that there was a conspiracy of silence
within our community. We used to say, "You don't reform apartheid, you get rid of
it."

      In 1982, I learned my name was on the list for assassination plans of
all political activists in the country. One day I was driving to visit my father. I
arrived at a T-junction. That was the last thing I remember. I woke up in an
intensive care unit after twelve days out. I had eleven stab wounds. The doctors
were worried that my assassins would return to finish the job. The security police
came to look for me because they realized I had been rescued. They looked at all
hospitals in the area where black people could be taken. The doctor moved me
to a coloured hospital. That was how rooted apartheid was in South Africa. The
police never thought to look for me there.

      By 1985, my younger brother had become a poet of the struggle. We
went to the funeral of an eleven-year-old girl who was killed by a tear gas canister.
All funerals were platforms for political speeches to rally the people. Ten thousand
attended. Before long, the police came, as they often did. They said we had three
minutes to disperse. But they couldn't count the time. After 90 seconds, all hell
broke loose. In the next 45 seconds, it was silent. Four bodies lay on the ground.
One was my brother. The response of the investigative commission was that the
police acted under extreme provocation, and they couldn't be blamed for his death.

      1985 was also the year I performed *Miss Julie* with Sandra Prinsloo at
the Market Street Theatre. The play was about a white woman who seduces her
servant. When we kissed, 200 people marched out in protest, all white. In 1987, I
did *Othello*. I was the first black Othello in South Africa. The street was lined with
white people trying to kill me. Protesters called me a terrorist masquerading as
an artist. These things only served to strengthen my determination and resolve.

      In 1990, Mandela[2] was released. He came out of prison when we
were teetering on open warfare, and we were all shocked when he proposed
negotiation. We weren't interested in negotiations. We were planning tribunals,
prosecutions, Nuremberg trials. We wanted physical retribution. We wanted to
see people in jail. We wanted our turn. We were going to set up killer squads to

---

[2] Nelson Mandela was the first democratically elected President of South Africa, serving
from 1994 to 1999.

hunt them down. We thought this old man was senile. Mandela was a myth, a name, an embodiment of our struggle. I had met Mbeki,[3] we knew he was flesh, but Mandela was a ghost. When the world saw him on TV, what you don't realize is that was also the first time we saw what he looked like too. We knew it was Nelson only because he stood next to Winnie.

In 1995, Mandela announced that April 27, 1994 would be the election date. I went to the voting booths, stood in the queue for four hours. I brought my family, even the youngsters. I wanted the younger ones to experience that day, to take a photograph with their minds. Here was history, and we were living it. I went in, put a cross next to Nelson Mandela, and dropped the ballot into a stupid little box. When I left, I was annoyed. How can that be all it takes? Surely voting must be difficult? Just a simple stupid cross and a little box. Why did it take so long, if it was so easy?

In 1995, Mandela and Archbishop Tutu[4] wanted to put on a Truth and Reconciliation Commission ["TRC"]. If they had put the proposal on the ballot, there would have been no TRC. The majority of blacks would have wanted trials. The decision didn't belong to the people. We discovered the TRC had no prosecution powers. By coming forward and making confessions, you were exonerated of your crimes simply because you exposed the bloody truth. And these were the foot soldiers, not the big guys going before the TRC. De Klerk[5] apologized for the top government. Mbeki apologized for the liberation movement. All it took were apologies, and everything was forgotten without any sense of forgiveness.

I wondered if I should go before the Commission in order to find out who shot my brother. I wondered whether I should go because I too was attacked. But the way the TRC worked was this: a man could come to the TRC, say he was sorry he shot my brother and go free. Then I must look at that man and smile and call him my African brother. I knew [my brother's killer] was a white man, and for me, all white men became my brother's murderer because I didn't know which one had shot him. I decided not to go.

In 2000, I wrote a letter to my brother. I was very uncomfortable going to his grave because when I went, anger surged within me, and the need for revenge swelled. I constantly questioned if I made the right choice not to go to the TRC. The letter ended up becoming a play called *Nothing but the Truth*. In the end, I

---

[3] Thabo Mbeki was President of South Africa from 1999 to 2008.

[4] Archbishop Desmond Tutu chaired South Africa's TRC, and was awarded the Nobel Peace Prize in 1984.

[5] F.W. de Klerk was the last apartheid-era President of South Africa, serving from 1989 to 1994. Along with Nelson Mandela, he won the Nobel Peace Prize in 1993.

came out on the other side a better man. I give thanks to my brother for paying the ultimate price for the freedom I am enjoying, for the freedom my children are enjoying.

We came to understand the necessity of the TRC. But, as individuals, we carried with us a great pain. There was no therapy for the victims of violence. We were left to heal ourselves, to fight out our own demons and devils, our anger, bitterness, and hurt. But you have to balance this with the good that came for the country, to be able to forgive yourself and your country. Everything has one moment in life, and like an actor on the stage about to deliver the most important line, there's a breath that if you miss it, the words become . . . a bland line.

If prosecutions happened in 1994, I would have supported that. Now, we're too far down the road of reconciliation. What would we gain now from prosecutions? We need more jobs, more investment, more schools. We need to focus on economic empowerment with a preference for the formerly marginalized. It's not only the responsibility of the government, but private and civil society must be active as well. Otherwise, in twenty years or 40, there will be a new revolution of the unsatisfied black masses.

Prosecutions are too complicated for beautiful South Africa. Personally, I don't need prosecution of the man who shot my brother. He's suffered enough. He knows what he did. Retribution creates a struggle for those you punish—the end of your struggle becomes the beginning of their struggle. I'm not saying you should forget the past. You should use the past as reference, lest you forget.

CHAPTER 1

South Africa's Ongoing Pursuit of Justice

*It was very interesting for me [to represent people seeking amnesty at the TRC];
it was a huge eye opener. In the initial rounds we helped them with their
applications. All they had to do was disclose all the acts they were involved in.
Interestingly enough, we had anticipated that communities were going to be quite
conflicted during the hearings for amnesties, but we were pleasantly surprised,
considering [that] we were acting for the applicants. [In one case] the families
of the victims were so forgiving; they physically got up and hugged [our client]. I
was sitting there with my mouth wide open. This was one of the positive things
about the TRC. Tutu's statement, "There is potential in all of us to be saints," was
a tangible thing I saw on that day.*

Anonymous, Instructor of Law
Durban, January 2007

In 1994, South Africa's first democratic election sounded the
death knell of the apartheid State. A nation torn apart by systematic racial
discrimination, oppression, and violence began a journey toward justice,
equality, and reconciliation that continues to this day. For years, South Africa's
transition has been hailed as a model of success. The Truth and Reconciliation
Commission ("TRC"), designed to reveal truths about the past by offering
individualized amnesty to perpetrators of apartheid-era crimes in exchange

for full disclosure about their politically-motivated abuses, was a major part of the lore of the South African miracle. More than a decade after those first democratic elections, however, a growing literature that reexamines the transition has emerged. The prosecution of apartheid-era crimes is part of that reassessment. The TRC's work, for example, did not resolve the issue of prosecutions of perpetrators who refused to participate in the TRC or were denied amnesty. Although the TRC operated on the premise that those who were not granted amnesty would face legal justice, few prosecutions for apartheid-era crimes have in fact occurred.

The issue of prosecutions is in some ways straightforward, in other ways dauntingly complex. On the one hand, refusing to prosecute anyone is anathema to international human rights obligations to hold perpetrators accountable and to prevent impunity for egregious abuses of fundamental freedoms. On the other hand, implementing this obligation raises a series of difficult practical and political questions. South Africans routinely express both faith and skepticism, often in the same breath, about the potential of prosecutions. John Kani, one of the country's most respected writers and performers, captures this contradiction in the Prologue, recounting his personal struggle with apartheid's brutalities and the political and legal efforts to pursue justice in its aftermath. He narrates a painful history, contemplates the legitimacy of prosecutions and different notions of justice, and questions the utility of holding abusers to account, all while attempting to balance the present and future needs of his country, his family, and himself. Kani answers the question of whether to pursue prosecutions in his "beautiful South Africa" with an emphatic, "No, not now." However, his view is only one amongst a remarkable diversity of perspectives. Others, such as Yasmin Sooka, a former TRC Commissioner, assert just as emphatically, "Yes, we still need prosecutions."

The Reflections in this volume embrace these debates and examine where a cross-section of South Africans stand—politically, legally, and emotionally—on the issue of apartheid-era prosecutions. Faced with the lapse of time and varying estimations of the progress already achieved, South Africans now confront challenging questions concerning the appropriateness and desired nature of further prosecutions. Will prosecutions foster reconciliation and entrench the rule of law, or instead exacerbate past and current divisions? Are prosecutions of a small number of perpetrators the best way to achieve justice, or would justice be better served by investing resources to address the broader structural legacy of apartheid? Must South Africa choose between criminal justice and restorative justice, or can prosecutions be conceived and structured to promote forgiveness and reconciliation that supports social transformation? If prosecutions are desirable, who should be prosecuted, and for what acts?

These questions permeate this work and reappear from different temporal perspectives as well as through different individuals' eyes and memories. Chapter 2 provides a historical perspective on the TRC, with a focus on the work of its Amnesty Committee and its "unfinished business." Chapter 3 then outlines the prosecutions powers of the National Prosecuting Authority ("NPA"), including prosecutorial discretion and the 2005 amended guidelines, and analyzes them in light of a constitutional challenge launched against the policy. Chapter 4 examines the prosecutions policy at work both during the TRC process and after, carefully scrutinizing the application of the amended guidelines through the lens of two important cases, one well known against Adriaan Vlok[6] for the attempted murder of Frank Chikane,[7] and the other virtually unknown against the Azanian People's Liberation Army ("APLA") Four.[8] Finally, Chapter 5 considers the voices of South Africans to offer lessons learned from the past and possible ways forward, including an examination of whether a new national dialogue on prosecutions offers transformative opportunities to address unresolved issues from the TRC.

Personal narratives drawn from interviews are interspersed between and within the chapters to offer diverse South African viewpoints on prosecutions. Taken together, these Reflections present disparate yet intertwined perspectives that reveal lingering tensions and possible directions for the future. These narratives animate a series of emerging themes and debates that inform the recurring questions surrounding prosecutions of apartheid-era crimes:

1. *Prosecutions are required to uphold the rule of law.* This issue has generated controversy among lawyers, academics, victims, and politicians. In 1996, the Constitutional Court upheld the constitutionality of the TRC's conditional, individualized amnesty on the grounds that it preserved victims' rights to pursue prosecutions

---

[6] Adriaan Vlok was the Minister of Law and Order in apartheid South Africa from 1986 to 1991.

[7] Frank Chikane was a prominent anti-apartheid activist and the former head of the South African Council of Churches. He also served in the African National Congress ("ANC") government under President Mbeki.

[8] APLA was the armed wing of the Pan-Africanist Congress of Azania ("PAC"), one of the major anti-apartheid groups in South Africa.

of anyone who failed to appear before the TRC or was denied amnesty. Some argue that this promise—that the TRC was a necessary compromise at a unique and critical moment in South Africa's history, but that ultimately the rule of law would be enforced—prohibits the government from declining to pursue further prosecutions. Adding another layer of complexity is the issue of prosecutorial discretion. In 2005, the NPA promulgated new guidelines that specifically address apartheid-era prosecutions. This amended prosecutions policy reaffirmed the NPA's existing authority to enter into plea bargains with defendants in exchange for information, and provided a set of criteria to guide decisions about whether or not to prosecute individual apartheid-era perpetrators. The policy reinvigorated the underlying debate about the propriety of amnesty for human rights abuses. Although the NPA's amended policy recognized that a mere continuation of the TRC's amnesty process would violate victims' rights and would be inconsistent with the objectives of the TRC, many South Africans have worried that the amended prosecutions policy was tantamount to a second amnesty. As discussed in detail in Chapter 3, a constitutional challenge to the amended prosecutions policy argued that failure to prosecute apartheid-era crimes violates South Africa's obligations, as enshrined in its constitution and customary international law, to investigate, prosecute, and punish violations of human rights. In December 2008, the Pretoria High Court declared the amended policy unconstitutional. Nevertheless, the debate will certainly continue: are prosecutions necessary to prevent impunity? Will prosecutions successfully bolster public confidence in the State's commitment to justice and convince people that the legal system works for them? Does South Africa have a legal duty to prosecute under international law? What level of prosecutorial discretion is appropriate?

2. *Prosecutions fit into some visions of justice—but not others.* Justice in South Africa has many different meanings. For a mother still searching for the remains of her murdered child, justice may mean locating the body to hold a proper burial. While a torture victim may demand purely retributive justice—the punishment of the torturer— justice for human rights attorneys may involve legal accountability for those higher up the chain of command. For former soldiers, justice may come in the form of an apology from superiors who sent them

to fight but later refused to take responsibility for the consequences of their orders. For marginalized communities, justice may be restorative, in the form of development funding and reparations, or justice may mean a renewed commitment to dealing with crime, corruption, and racial tension. How should prosecutions negotiate these different visions of justice?

3. *Prosecutions as a destabilizing force to society versus prosecutions as a benefit to individuals' pursuit of justice.* Opponents of prosecutions often express concern that pursuing prosecutions will do more harm than good by re-establishing old divisions and opening healed wounds. There is a temporal component to this debate as well. Some feel that prosecutions early on in the transition would have been counterproductive, while others feel the threat of prosecutions would have effectively motivated more individuals to come forward and participate in the TRC process. Some believe that prosecutions even at this late date could still prove destabilizing; others do not fear instability but rather wish to look forward rather than backward. Some assert that true progress cannot be made until justice is served for the crimes of the past and perpetrators are held to account. Under this construct, prosecutions are relevant both on the societal level by emphasizing the rule of law, as well as on the individual level by achieving justice for individual victims. Do the benefits of pursuing prosecutions outweigh the risks? Has the window of opportunity to pursue prosecutions closed because the country is truly on the road to reconciliation, or can a reconciled South Africa only emerge if law is used to prevent impunity? Are individual victims' rights to redress being adequately taken into consideration?

4. *Prosecutions raise questions of evenhandedness.* If prosecutions are pursued in South Africa, a threshold question to be answered remains, "whom do you prosecute?" The desire for evenhandedness is often highlighted, but evenhandedness has many interpretations. For some, it means that going forward there should be equal numbers of prosecutions of former apartheid State and liberation forces. For others, it means that the apartheid State that was responsible for the majority of atrocities should be the target of the majority of prosecutions. Still others focus on the need to prosecute people who set policy and made decisions rather than low-level actors who

carried out orders from above. Which idea of evenhandedness best serves South Africa's varied interests? Is it acceptable or desirable to prosecute low-level perpetrators if those are the actors against whom evidence can be brought, or does justice require tracing accountability up the chain of command?

5. *Prosecutions raise resource allocation questions when there are competing societal priorities.* It is sometimes argued that resources that could be allocated to prosecutions would be better spent remedying the structural legacy of apartheid—for example, by building infrastructure and social programs to serve entire communities that continue to suffer from poverty, unemployment, and crime. Others assert that, despite South Africa's limited resources, courtroom justice is too important to forgo and must be prioritized to ensure the rule of law and individual rights to redress. Can the resources be found to pursue both goals simultaneously? If not, is the need for investment in education, housing, HIV/AIDS treatment, and other social programs so great that these goals must be prioritized over investigations of the past? Should law enforcement resources be spent on current crime prevention and policing or on apartheid-era criminal investigations?

6. *Prosecutions highlight the strengths and weaknesses of a court-centric approach.* Many victims who desire prosecutions do so at least in part because they want to know the truth about what happened to them or their loved ones—who the direct perpetrators were, where and how the violations took place, and who set the policy or gave the order that led to the violation. Criminal investigations and prosecutions may provide valuable insights into details about particular cases. Court proceedings, however, may not be the best vehicle to uncover the truth, since it is generally in the defendant's interest to deny guilt in order to evade culpability. In addition, prosecutions are constrained by the legal requirements that, for example, evidence be admissible in court and sufficient to prove guilt beyond a reasonable doubt. Are there better ways to help victims find closure and a sense of justice than through criminal prosecutions? Are there significant demonstrative benefits to society in prosecuting those cases, even if limited in number, in which there is sufficient evidence to secure a conviction?

7. *Prosecutions could provide new opportunities for transformation within society.* Connected to the principle of *ubuntu*[9]—the African idea that one's humanity is tied to the humanity of others—is a belief that prosecutions for apartheid-era human rights violations in South Africa might achieve a kind of restorative justice that would help heal old rifts rather than reopen such wounds. While prosecutions are traditionally associated with criminal proceedings, some interviewees encouraged thinking outside this traditional paradigm when considering what prosecutions can achieve. By separating prosecutions from individual imprisonment and punishment, a restorative vision could, for example, tie prosecutions to the issue of reparations for damage entire communities suffered as a result of apartheid-era policies and practices. Could prosecutions be used as a catalyst for reparations or other broader effort to address communal concerns, thereby allowing prosecutions to have a healing effect, including for those victims whose cases cannot be prosecuted? Does the potential for community healing change the balance of benefits versus risks discussed above?

The plethora of issues and insights in the Reflections offer a rich opportunity for new solutions in South Africa and beyond. The narrative that follows this chapter from Ilan Lax, a former TRC staffer and attorney, launches the discussion and captures the array of debates: he highlights the ongoing tensions between legal principles, political reality, and power—both within society and within himself. These themes not only inform discussions in South Africa but speak more generally to the decisions that transitional societies must face regarding prosecutions. Since South Africa has served as a model for transitional justice efforts around the globe, its lessons and ongoing struggles with the question of prosecutions can also guide other societies as they seek to uphold the rule of law and achieve reconciliation and justice.

---

[9] One of the founding principles of the new South Africa, *ubuntu* refers to a spirit of community and togetherness, or the concept that one's humanity is tied to the humanity of others. Nelson Mandela has described *ubuntu* as a quality of mutual responsibility and compassion, or the idea that "a person is a person because of other people." Desmond Tutu has explained that *ubuntu* "refers to gentleness, to compassion, to hospitality, to openness to others, to vulnerability, to be available to others and to know that you are bound up with them in the bundle of life." Anthony Sampson, *Mandela: The Authorized Biography* (New York: Knopf, 1999).

REFLECTION

"Anyone who says applying for amnesty was easy or a soft option is wrong. Many who applied were as broken as the victims of their acts."

Ilan Lax, Former TRC Staffer, Attorney
Pietermaritzburg, January 2007

I was born in Israel. My parents had emigrated there from South Africa, and they returned to South Africa when I was about a year-and-a-half. Growing up, I was subjected to a lot of anti-Semitism, so I began to understand what it is to be the underdog, to be on the receiving end of prejudice and hatred. By the time I'd finished school, I didn't have money to go to university. I had a July call-up pending to be conscripted into the SADF [South African Defence Force]. Interestingly enough, I came out of [military service] much more politically aware than when I came in, for two reasons: one, I was confronted with a lot of anti-Semitism in the army; two, I saw the way the coloured and black troops were treated. I thought, "Hey, these guys are going to die with the rest [of us]; they are putting their lives on the line . . . yet they are being treated as second class people." And that just didn't seem right.

In March 1986, I started a law practice in Pietermaritzburg with two of my friends. As far as we know, it was the first non-racial legal firm in Pietermaritzburg. Some people thought we were really crazy, but to us it was quite normal. We were friends, and we wanted to practice together, so we did. I focused primarily on human rights work, from land rights issues to detention without trial issues. I was acting chairperson of [the Detainee Support Committee for Pietermaritzburg and surrounding areas] for a number of years. I say acting chairperson because no one took a permanent chairmanship position, otherwise you'd be immediately arrested and detained. For ten years we ran that practice until I joined the Truth Commission in 1996. I initially took just a year's leave of absence from that practice, but that year [at the TRC] stretched into five and a half years.

I was selected to the [TRC's] Human Rights Violations Committee initially and then later to the Amnesty Committee. I think that working on those two Committees gave me a unique perspective on the TRC process because I also understood the Human Rights Violations [Committee] process, the victims' side of things.

I think the amnesty process was very effective in the long term. Once the parties agreed to the idea of amnesty, then the question was what kind of amnesty it would be. It was clear that this would be a voluntary, due process kind of amnesty. A lot of people say, "Why didn't you make findings about all sorts of other people?" And I say, "Because they didn't come to the Commission." We didn't have any jurisdiction over them, because the Commission didn't have its own jurisdiction. It only dealt with people who came to it on a voluntary basis. We weren't a court of law; we weren't a prosecuting agency; we weren't an investigative unit in that sense. The TRC was a creature of statute, and only had those powers inherent in the statute.

Anyone who says applying for amnesty was easy or a soft option is wrong. Many who applied were as broken as the victims of their acts. In many cases survivors were much more whole than the perpetrators. These perpetrators often no longer had their families; they had post-traumatic stress disorder and were pariahs in their own communities. Someone who had worked with de Kock[10] was a deacon in his church! His own family didn't know he was a killer. But at a certain level, I wished there was a way to grant conditional amnesty, so that it would require one or two acts of penance or reparation. But can you imagine the administrative nightmare that would pose? And how do you prosecute people afterwards?

[Prosecution] was not part of our jurisdiction. The TRC only had power to recommend this to the State. That has to come from a broader social compact; it was the State's role to back up prosecutions as a real possibility. Perpetrators had a choice to make a full disclosure or not, and this choice was affected by the possibility of prosecutions. There had to be sticks as well as carrots, and the stick was so slow in coming that it actually undermined the work of the TRC. Prosecutions should have been happening while the Commission was ongoing. We consciously decided to use our discretion under Section 19 to hold inquiries and have *in camera* hearings,[11] essentially to make people afraid so they'd think seriously about applying for amnesty. We targeted cliques of powerful people as well as foot soldiers. But the decision to prosecute or not to prosecute was the prerogative of the State.

You can't see the TRC in isolation. The TRC is just one pillar of the transformation; the other pillars are democratization, the RDP

---

[10] Eugene de Kock was the commander of the notorious Vlakplaas unit of the South African Police ("SAP") during the apartheid years, which targeted and murdered numerous anti-apartheid activities.

[11] Section 19 of the TRC's enabling act granted the TRC authority to investigate amnesty applications. *In camera*, the Latin for "in chambers," refers to hearings conducted in private.

[Reconstruction and Development Programme], welfare structures, economic changes including BEE [Black Economic Empowerment Programme], and affirmative action. These all need to happen at a similar pace and time.

I'm torn between two positions. The broader, human [rights] orientated part of me says in order to respect the institution of the Truth Commission and the promise and expectation that was implicit in the settlement, you have to prosecute people. And I believe you should prosecute those most responsible. So let's ask ourselves this question: if you were going to prosecute those most responsible, who's left to prosecute? There are a couple of generals that are still left alive. Some of them are already in their 70s, so you choose some of those generals maybe, if you have enough evidence on them. Remember that the evidence they have is primarily on the lower to middle-order people; they don't have a lot of evidence on the generals, otherwise they would have prosecuted them a long time ago. But to prosecute a bunch of foot soldiers at this point in time is meaningless.

Bear in mind that quite a lot of liberation movement people didn't apply for amnesty. So the point is this: if you prosecute Mphahlele,[12] you may have to make sure you prosecute someone of an equivalent rank [on the State side] if you want the process to be seen to be fair. You don't want to end up victimizing people in what appears to be a witch-hunt, because what possible public good would that serve? A witch-hunt will serve no good at all; it will simply polarize the situation further. So if you are going to have prosecutions it has to be done on an evenhanded basis, with people from all ranks being prosecuted at the same time.

[But] on the other hand, I don't see the point. Our courts can't even deal with the crime that is happening now. We can't properly police it, investigate it, or prosecute it to fruition. Our conviction rate is so small; it is something like 2%, just of ordinary crime. How on earth can we deal with a mass of criminal political prosecutions, for political crimes? And which courts are going to deal with it? Are you going to put a whole lot of other cases on hold while we deal with this? There is a queue of [standard criminal] cases, and the delay on prosecutions is enormous. I don't know whether it is worth

---

[12] Letlapa Mphahlele is a PAC leader who ordered several attacks against civilians during the struggle between the liberation movements and the apartheid state including, most notoriously, the bombing at St. James Church on July 25, 1993 in which eleven congregants were killed and another 58 wounded, as well as an attack at the Heidelberg Tavern on December 23, 1993 in which five people were killed. Presentation by Ginn Fourie and Letlapa Mphahlele, Books Building Brides Function in Celebration of a Decade of Democracy, April 19, 2004, http://www.fs.gov.za/Departments/SAC/Library/jul-sept2004_main_article-books%20that%20brought%20enemies%20together.htm.

it. In light of all those things I have mentioned, it is highly unlikely that we will see high-ranking prosecutions. So while part of me says you have to do it, then part of me says if you do it and fail, then what?

Just because a perpetrator [who didn't receive or request amnesty] is not punished doesn't mean full impunity exists. I like to think of transformative justice, which is a combination of restorative justice and truth. A truth commission is not an adversarial process. The amnesty applications weren't meant to be as adversarial as some of them ended up being but because you had judges steeped in adversarial tradition, it was very hard to have it any other way.

The lawyers were largely steeped in an adversarial tradition [as well]. Very few of the lawyers who appeared before the Commission had any background in non-adversarial processes, ADR [alternative dispute resolution] processes, they didn't know how to behave in a non-adversarial way. I understood that in an ADR process, restorative justice is much more feasible and attainable. I think it is still possible now. I think that would be much more beneficial [to] look at an alternative process wherein [the government prosecution] guidelines are amended to force people into a restorative justice track, that allows for victim-offender mediation, that allows for a kind of quasi-truth commission. It doesn't have to be a truth commission, but it can be a process in which people can at least begin to understand one another in a way that builds communities. So if a chief in KZN [KwaZulu-Natal] is known to have been a warlord, at least he or she could be brought into a process in which they engage with the victims of their community who became refugees. And maybe that rift is healed. Maybe that is a better process that the State could engage in as part of the legacy of the Truth Commission, as part of the reparation measures. Maybe [the State would] rather sponsor that than waste millions and millions of rand on prosecutions that may not be successful.

You don't necessarily need the threat of prosecution in the background to get people into the process. People have a need to heal. Even if you are a perpetrator ... living with what you have done, you need to be unburdened of that at some point. All of us as human beings need that. There is the example of Brian Mitchell,[13] who raised money for the Trust Feed community. In his

---

[13] Mitchell is a former apartheid-era policeman. In 1992, he was sentenced to 30 years imprisonment for his role in the 1988 murder of eleven residents, mainly women and children, of the Trust Feed community in Pietermaritzburg, KwaZulu-Natal. Mitchell's 30-year prison sentence was expunged after he testified before the TRC's Amnesty Committee. He subsequently apologized to the community and has made efforts to contribute to its economic and social development.

own way, he has done something concrete about the problem. Some people get by on hatred and that's their bundle, but they are relatively few in the broader spectrum of humanity. Everyone has that capacity, but by and large most people want to let go of that stuff so they can move on with their lives. That was the abiding motivation among so many perpetrators who came [to the TRC]. They weren't afraid of prosecutions. They wanted to be united back with their communities, to stop being outsiders. What could be a driving force is that if you can bring in enough credible people to begin to promote that approach and if it can be piloted and can be seen to work, maybe the fact that it does work will bring others in. So maybe that is a positive way of moving forward in a restorative justice mode at a community level.

CHAPTER 2

The TRC and Its Unfinished Business

How do we balance [the interests of] the perpetrators who want to be assured that nothing will happen to them and [the interests of] the community that has suffered and wants a better life? The one way that we can achieve that balance is by having both come together and work on it.

Ela Gandhi, Peace Activist, Former Member of Parliament
Durban, January 2007

I. INTRODUCTION

The TRC and the question of prosecutions are inextricably linked in South Africa. This was as true in the immediate wake of the transition to democracy as it is fifteen years after the end of apartheid. The TRC was intended to bridge South Africa's past and future, but it was never designed as a complete replacement for prosecutions. In fact, in its Final Report, the TRC explicitly reminded the government that those who did not receive amnesty could be subject to prosecution. It provided a list of approximately 300 names to the NPA for further investigation and possible prosecution, and described cases of unsolved disappearances as "perhaps the most significant piece of unfinished business" of the TRC.[14]

Established by the National Unity and Reconciliation Act of 1995, the TRC received testimony from individual victims at public hearings between April 1996 and June 1997, and also conducted investigations, undertook research, and collected additional statements during that period. From the middle of 1997 through late 1998, the Commission shifted its focus to examine the motivation to commit gross human rights violations by exploring the context and causes of abuses, and by attempting to establish the political and moral accountability of both individuals and institutions. During this second phase, the Commission received submissions from political parties and other institutions, and also conducted amnesty hearings. The first five volumes of the Final Report were released in 1998, and were then supplemented with an additional two volumes in 2003 after the Amnesty Committee had evaluated all amnesty applications and completed its work.

Critics and commentators have debated the successes and shortcomings of the TRC in great detail. Prosecutions are one aspect of these debates. Indeed, the TRC and its unfinished business are omnipresent in discussions about prosecutions for apartheid-era crimes. In its Final Report, the Commission stated that Nuremberg-like trials were not an option for South Africa because the threat of prosecutions would have undermined the negotiated settlement that ended apartheid.[15] The TRC's Final Report allowed that: "It could be argued that the new government has an obligation, in terms of international law, to deal with those who were responsible for crimes committed under apartheid, even though their acts were considered legitimate by the South African government at the time."[16] The Final Report, however, did not recognize any specific obligation under international law to prosecute perpetrators because "the urgent need to promote reconciliation in South Africa demanded a different response, and that large-scale prosecution of apartheid criminals was not the route the country had chosen."[17]

In considering the prosecutions question, the TRC also observed that the judicial system lacked the time, money, and personnel to undertake

---

[14] "Report of the Human Rights Violations Committee," *Truth and Reconciliation Commission of South Africa Report* (2003), Volume 6, Section 4, Chapter 1, p. 532.

[15] "Foreword by Chairperson," *Truth and Reconciliation Commission of South Africa Report* (1998), Volume 1, Chapter 1, p. 5.

[16] "Findings and Recommendations," *Truth and Reconciliation Commission of South Africa Report* (2003), Volume 6, Section 5, Chapter 1, p. 594.

[17] *Ibid.*, p. 595.

widespread prosecutions during the transition to democracy.[18] It further noted that the criminal justice system is not well-suited to reveal the truth, and that legal proceedings can be a harrowing experience for victims forced to endure cross-examination.[19] Nevertheless, the volumes of the Final Report released in 2003 acknowledged that, while pervasive prosecutions during the first years of democracy could have compromised peace and taxed limited resources, "it has always been understood that, where amnesty has not been applied for, it is incumbent upon the present government to have a bold prosecution policy in order to avoid any suggestion of impunity or of contravening its obligations in terms of international law."[20]

The parameters of the TRC, as well as its mission and legacy, inform the broader debate about prosecutions. For example, the TRC did not provide for a blanket amnesty, but insisted on conditional, individualized amnesty—an exchange of full truth-telling to forgo prosecution. Just as importantly, only 1,160 individuals received amnesty from the TRC, so numerous perpetrators remain eligible for prosecution for crimes committed during the apartheid era. Many individuals did not participate in the TRC process, and thus have not been subjected to any formal accountability for apartheid-era crimes. There was a particular dearth in applications from high-ranking officials and leaders. The separate and important questions of whether and how prosecutions should be pursued against these individuals remain open, but the fact that the TRC did not deal with all perpetrators and abuses frames the attitudes of many toward prosecutions.

Narratives from members of Khulumani, a victims' support group, are interspersed throughout this chapter to demonstrate the diversity of attitudes about the TRC and its unfinished business. The narratives also reflect the interplay between different aspects of the TRC's mandate: to reveal the truth and offer a forum for victims to tell their stories, to acknowledge violations and make reparations for suffering, and to grant amnesty in exchange for full disclosure. As these Reflections indicate, while the TRC is often perceived as successfully revealing unknown truths, it initiated but did not complete the process of reconciliation. Some believe strongly that trials are required to fulfill the promise of the TRC. Proponents of trials assert that prosecutions would demonstrate that those who did not seek amnesty before the TRC

---

[18] "Foreword by Chairperson," *Truth and Reconciliation Commission of South Africa Report* (1998), Volume 1, Chapter 1, p. 5.

[19] *Ibid.*, pp. 5-6.

[20] "Findings and Recommendations," *Truth and Reconciliation Commission of South Africa Report* (2003), Volume 6, Section 5, Chapter 1, p. 595.

cannot escape with impunity, while also providing a powerful catalyst towards repentance and reconciliation. Others, in contrast, desire monetary reparations more than guilty verdicts, and believe that reconciliation demands that those who remain marginalized be offered social benefits to support upward mobility, as well as a voice in the political process.

II. THE TRC MANDATE

The TRC was created in 1995 to help South Africa answer a critical question: where do we go from here? After a history laden with lies and misrepresentations, the TRC promised that truths would be revealed. Debts accumulated over years of exclusion, oppression, and inequality would be repaid. The architects and operators of a political system and security apparatus intended to deprive an entire population of its humanity and dignity would be called upon to acknowledge their role. The TRC was premised on the assumption that the country could only survive if it honestly confronted its painful past, and the hope that the challenging process of uncovering and documenting the truth might lead to some measure of national reconciliation. The ANC leadership, having negotiated a tenuous peace with the former apartheid government and having crafted an Interim Constitution, envisioned the TRC as a process that would allow the country to examine its history while building a more just and democratic future. Those who conceived of the TRC[21] recognized the political reality that developing South Africa's new future required considerable compromise. Immediate stability and future prosperity were thought to preclude retributive punishment in the transition from apartheid to democratically-elected government.

The TRC's mission was enormous: to establish as complete a picture as possible of the causes, nature, and extent of gross human rights violations committed during the apartheid era; to facilitate the granting of amnesty to those who made a full disclosure of politically-motivated crimes; and to restore the dignity of victims by offering a forum to tell their story, granting reparations for their suffering, and establishing the fate of those whose whereabouts remained unknown. It simultaneously provided a space where perpetrators, without any obligation to seek forgiveness or express regret, might obtain amnesty in exchange for fully revealing the atrocities they had

---

[21] The most prominent supporters of a TRC included human rights and labor law professor Kader Asmal, President of the Methodist Church of South Africa and anti-apartheid Member of Parliament Alex Boraine, Nelson Mandela, and Archbishop Desmond Tutu.

committed. The process was limited in time and scope, focusing exclusively on politically-motivated crimes committed between March 1, 1960 and May 11, 1994.[22] The TRC also addressed only gross violations of human rights, defined as killings, abductions, torture, or severe ill-treatment, as well as any attempt, conspiracy, incitement, instigation, command, or procurement to commit such acts.

III. THE TRC AND THE CONSTITUTION

From the beginning, the TRC mandate was controversial. The debate about the TRC involved questions of principle, for example whether the TRC violated international obligations to prosecute gross violations of human rights. The controversy also precipitated cases brought by groups and individuals, for example challenging whether the TRC deprived victims of particular constitutionally-protected rights.

South Africa has often been hailed as a model for transitional societies rather than criticized as a failure to uphold the rule of law. However, customary international law indicates that a State has a duty to protect human rights by preventing wholesale impunity for certain abuses, although this obligation does not necessarily demand the prosecution of every human rights violation. The TRC's requirement of full disclosure in exchange for amnesty meant that perpetrators would be forced to confront their victims and face their own culpability, and therefore not escape with absolute impunity. Whether this suffices to meet international obligations remains an open controversy. On one side, some argue that: "If law is unavailable to punish widespread brutality of the recent past, what lesson can be offered for the future?"[23] In contrast, others assert that the value of prosecutions can be outweighed by the risk that they may destabilize a country. A fragile State should not be constrained by international law to undertake prosecutions that may lead to its collapse.

This debate over legal principles manifested itself in a variety of legal cases challenging the TRC during its brief existence. The constitutionality of granting amnesty (and waiving both civil and criminal liability) was challenged by three prominent victims' families, including the widow of Steve Biko, the

---

[22] Promotion of National Unity and Reconciliation Act (Act No. 34 of 1995), Chapter 4, Section 18.1. *See* Appendix B.

[23] Diane F. Orentlicher, "Settling Accounts: The Duty To Prosecute Human Rights Violations of a Prior Regime," *Yale Law Journal*, Vol. 100 (1991), p. 2542.

brother of Griffiths Mxenge, and the son of Fabian and Florence Ribeiro.[24] In *Azanian People's Organization (AZAPO) and Others v. The President of the Republic of South Africa and Others*,[25] the applicants argued that Section 20(7) of the TRC Act violated the Interim Constitution's requirement that individuals be allowed to bring cases before an "independent or impartial forum."

The Constitutional Court unanimously upheld the constitutionality of the TRC Act despite the fact that:

> The effect of an amnesty undoubtedly impacts upon very fundamental rights. All persons are entitled to the protection of the law against unlawful invasions of their right to life, their right to respect for and protection of dignity and their right not to be subject to torture of any kind. When those rights are invaded those aggrieved by such invasion have the right to obtain redress in the ordinary courts of law and those guilty of perpetrating such violations are answerable before such courts, both civilly and criminally. An amnesty to the wrongdoer effectively obliterates such rights.[26]

In determining that granting amnesty pursuant to the TRC Act was constitutional, the Court relied on the importance of uncovering the truth and the fact that a perpetrator could face civil and criminal charges if he failed to satisfy the TRC's amnesty requirements; thus, victims were not absolutely deprived of the right to prosecution.

> That truth, which the victims of repression seek so desperately to know is, in the circumstances, much more likely to be forthcoming if those responsible for such monstrous misdeeds are encouraged to disclose the whole truth with the incentive that they will not receive the punishment which they undoubtedly deserve if they do. . . . With that incentive, what might unfold are objectives fundamental to the ethos of a new

---

[24] Black Consciousness leader Steve Biko was killed in police custody from brutal blows to the head in September 1977; Griffiths Mxenge, an attorney and anti-apartheid activist, was assassinated by state security forces in November 1981, and his body severely mutilated; Fabian and Florence Ribeiro, who documented brutality and abuses suffered by black South Africans, were gunned down outside their home by state agents in December 1986.

[25] *Azanian People's Organization (AZAPO) and Others v. The President of the Republic of South Africa and Others*, 1996 (4) SA 671 (Const. Ct.).

[26] *Ibid.*, para. 9.

constitutional order.[27]

Additional challenges materialized before the Commission released its Final Report in 1998. Former president de Klerk successfully sued to temporarily prevent the Commission from naming him for having known about several bombings, after the fact, but failing to report them. The ANC unsuccessfully attempted to block publication of the Final Report in its entirety because it was unhappy with the Commission's conclusions implicating the ANC in gross human rights violations. The Inkatha Freedom Party ("IFP") and SADF filed formal complaints with the Public Protector concerning what they perceived to be disparate treatment before the Commission.[28]

These court challenges resulted in foundational Constitutional Court decisions that understand the TRC amnesty process as a one-time event at a critical and unique moment in South Africa's history. The South African Constitution requires that "every court must prefer any reasonable interpretation of the legislation that is consistent with international law over any alternative interpretation that is inconsistent with international law."[29] Additionally, the Constitution requires that South Africa comply with customary international law, except when it contravenes the Constitution or an Act of Parliament.[30] Amnesty was the cornerstone of the negotiated transition to majority rule, and the TRC required victims to forgo certain rights in order to advance national unity and reconciliation. However, the Constitution and Constitutional Court decisions make clear that the State is still required to uphold its obligations under customary international law and to take all reasonable steps to prosecute perpetrators who did not receive amnesty. Any post-TRC process that offers amnesty to perpetrators of apartheid-era crimes would violate not only South Africa's international legal obligations but also the legacy of the TRC, which justified the use of conditional, individualized amnesty with the promise of prosecutions for those who did not come forward with the full truth.

---

[27] *Ibid.*, para. 17.

[28] For a detailed description of these and other legal challenges to the TRC, see "Legal Challenges," *Truth and Reconciliation Commission of South Africa Report* (1998), Volume 1, Chapter 7, and "Legal Challenges," *Truth and Reconciliation Commission of South Africa Report* (2003), Volume 6, Section 1, Chapter 4.

[29] Constitution of the Republic of South Africa (Act No. 108 of 1996).

[30] *Ibid.*, art. 232.

IV. THE TRC AT WORK

During a three-year period, the TRC took testimony from over 21,000 victims and witnesses, of whom approximately 2,000 testified publicly. Commissioners read an additional 18,000 written testimonials and evaluated over 7,000 amnesty applications. The TRC's Final Report narrates a significant part of South African history, much of which was previously undocumented and unknown. The report also makes extensive recommendations to the government, imploring political leaders to aid victims through monetary reparations and rehabilitation, and suggesting prosecutions of perpetrators who failed to seek or were denied amnesty. Still, as successful and internationally renowned as the TRC was, the narrative of Noluntu Sbukwana illustrates the immensity of the challenge of reaching all those affected by apartheid.

> *I am a Xhosa from the Eastern Cape, and I was traditionally married in 1995. My husband and I moved to an informal settlement in Soweto because he was a worker in the mines. Six months ago, he got sick, resigned from his position, and then died. He received a small package after he resigned, but if he died while he was still working, I would have received a pension. Now, I do not work; I do washing in the township and sometimes around here to make some money. I have three children, aged three, four, and eleven.*
>
> *In 1990, when I was sixteen years old, my brothers, Thembile and Yandisa Nthonti, were killed in KwaZulu-Natal, an IFP stronghold. They were chased down and attacked and killed by an IFP mob, probably for speaking Xhosa. It is difficult to know exactly who did it and why. We reported the case to the police, but we did not really follow-up because people were being killed daily, and it would not help much to pursue the case. Besides, my family did not really know how to follow-up. And at that time, we could not have trusted the police. We just buried them.*
>
> *My first memory of the TRC was hearing about it on the radio, and then seeing hearings on the television. I only thought it was focused on Boers killing blacks. Even though I thought it was right that we were finding out about the truth, I did not really follow it because it was not very nice to watch the*

hearings.

My family was not approached to go to the TRC, and I don't know anyone who participated in it. It was a good process, but it would not have worked for my family as the deaths of my brothers were so long ago. We did not even think about going to the TRC because what happened to my brothers was in the past, and we wanted to stop thinking about it. If legal action could have been taken, that might have been better—to bring the people who killed my brothers to justice, to be punished. Bringing people to the TRC was not going to help us obtain justice. Justice is a good thing, and I feel really bad about what happened to my brothers, but so much time has passed that I don't really have feelings left [to make me want to pursue it].

If the government can follow-up on prosecutions, then it is fine to try to bring people to justice. But I also think it should focus on other, more important priorities, like providing jobs for all people, proper housing, and increasing the visibility of the police in order to overcome crime. Jobs are extremely important now. My concern is that people have a good life.

Noluntu Sbukwana
Domestic
Soweto, October 2006

For Noluntu Sbukwana, the TRC and its three committees—one for human rights violations, one for reparations and rehabilitation, and one for assessing amnesty applications—meant little at the time. However, for others like Johannes Titus, whose narrative follows, the Commission played a vital role, both in terms of what it achieved and what it did not.

In 1976, I was sixteen years old. At Hanover Park, they shot at me from a truck. I was shot by the army with an R1.[31] When the bullet went inside, it opened a hole inside, and everything went outside. I went first to the morgue and didn't know I was there. [Eventually I was taken to Victoria Hospital.] I was very sick at the time, urgently, in a coma, and I didn't know whether I would survive. There were eight operations,

---

[31] This is the name for the South African-produced 7.62mm FN-FAL rifle used by the SADF from the 1960s through the 1990s.

*but one wound couldn't close properly. Every time, there was
swelling. I went to Groote Schuur [Hospital] to close the wound.
Afterwards, I was suffering constantly. I had a case, and Dullah
Omar[32] was my lawyer. I was suffering every day, the pain kept
coming, and they can't do any more operations. Every time I get
sick, I go back, and the hospital can't help.*

*The man who shot me came to tell my mother he was
sorry when I was in the hospital. She did not accept his apology.
He didn't go to the TRC, didn't get amnesty. [But through the
TRC process], Tutu and Boraine helped me.[33] I got an interim
ZAR 5,700 for reparations. ZAR 850 a month I get now; the
rent is ZAR 300, and the heater has to be on 24 hours a day. I
want help from the government, for my wife, my kids. She takes
care of me all the time.*

*The man who shot me, I forgave him in front of Tutu. I
don't know what he looks like, but I know he's white. I told my
mother she had to forgive him too. Every day, part of me is in
the graveyard because I don't know if I will survive. Every day, I
thank the Lord that I am still alive.*

Johannes Titus
Khulumani Support Group
Cape Town, October 2006

A. The Human Rights Violations Committee

The Human Rights Violations Committee of the TRC received and
documented testimony from individuals victimized by the State or by other
political groups during the course of the conflict. It compiled and clarified the
historical record, providing a comprehensive picture of the nature and types of
human rights violations committed. The Committee was charged to "establish
and make known the fate or whereabouts of victims," which was understood
to be essential to restore dignity to victims.[34] When the Committee found that

---

[32] Dullah Omar was an anti-apartheid activist and lawyer who served as the first Minister
of Justice under President Mandela, and later as Minister of Transport under President Mbeki.
[33] Archbishop Desmond Tutu served as Chair of the TRC, and Alex Boraine served as Deputy
Chair.
[34] Promotion of National Unity and Reconciliation Act (Act No. 34 of 1995), Chapter 2, Sec-

a gross violation had been committed with respect to a particular victim, it referred the case to the Committee on Reparation and Rehabilitation.

B. The Committee on Reparation and Rehabilitation

The TRC's Committee on Reparation and Rehabilitation was established to provide individual victims of gross human rights violations with some form of State-sponsored compensation for their suffering. It was charged with recommending approaches to rehabilitate and restore the human and civil dignity of victims.[35] The Committee ultimately recommended that a payment of ZAR 2.86 billion (US $328 million)[36] be divided among the victims of apartheid. It also suggested symbolic reparations such as monuments and holidays, as well as community and institutional reparations such as housing, education, and medical care. Finally, the Committee requested services to promote rehabilitation for the major psychological trauma that arose not only from apartheid-era abuses, but also from providing testimony before the TRC and from the emotional impact of seeing perpetrators walk free. In 2003, the government announced final reparations of ZAR 30,000 (approximately US $3,400) to each of 19,000 identified victims.[37]

The following narratives reveal that this sum was widely perceived as inadequate to either recognize the magnitude of suffering of victims or to make a tangible impact upon the quality of their lives, and remains a major source of dissatisfaction about the TRC's legacy. As Brian Mphahlele and Japhta Marawu explain, the insufficiency of reparations both disrespects their past suffering and reinforces a feeling of powerlessness and marginalization in the country they struggled to create.

> *I was arrested on January 10, 1977 for setting alight*
> *every government building in my community, Langa, in 1976.*
> *I was taken to Caledon Square[38] where I was brutally tortured*
> *for six days. My teeth were knocked out, I was electrocuted, but*

---

tions 3(1)(a-c).

[35] "Report of the Reparation and Rehabilitation Committee," *Truth and Reconciliation Commission of South Africa Report* (2003), Volume 6, Section 2, Chapter 1, p. 92.

[36] Estimates are based on May 2009 exchange rates.

[37] This sum was significantly lower than the ZAR 135,000 (approximately US $15,000) multi-year payment recommended by the TRC. Community and institutional reparations remain extremely limited.

[38] Caledon Square is the name of a police station in Cape Town.

I survived torture. Then I was transferred to Pollsmoor for six months in solitary confinement. I was in psychological torture, not allowed to speak to anyone, couldn't sing or whistle. After that I was transferred for a trial in camera.[39] *I was given five years. I was twenty years old and working with the PAC. I spent my 21st birthday in solitary confinement. I was classified in C group.*[40] *I had to be obedient to prison wardens, and I refused. I sustained internal head injuries from the torture, and I'm still on meds today. I'm suffering from amnesia; they did a scan at Groote Schuur [Hospital]. I tell my psychiatrist that I don't want to depend on drugs, but he said they are non-addictive.*

I went to the TRC in the 1990s to submit my statement. They asked, "What do you want us to do?" I said, "I need help." I didn't know about reparations. So they phoned the Trauma Centre in Woodstock, and I had four years of free counseling. I was called by the TRC again to say that they had too many cases, so I wouldn't be in a public hearing. I got interim reparations of 2,700 rand and spent it quickly because that's nothing. We fought for final reparations for years, waiting a long time, had demonstrations, and on April 15, [2003], the Khulumani executive committee went to hear this mean president talk about Volume Five of the Final Report. In the end, he said that all he'd pay out to all victims of gross human rights violations is a once-off payment.

Brian Mphahlele
Khulumani Support Group
Cape Town, October 2006

---

[39] *In camera*, the Latin for "in chambers," refers to legal proceedings which are conducted in private, outside the view of public observers.

[40] Apartheid-era classifications for prisoners determined everything from the number of letters the prisoner was allowed to write and receive each month (for C group, one each of no more than 500 words) to the number of visits per month (for C group, one visit with one person lasting no more than 45 minutes) to the type and quantity of food received at meals.

I was born in the struggle. My parents were too much involved. They were from Cape Town before the Group Areas Act,[41] and then they were displaced and moved. The struggle affected me so much that I had hatred for all white people. I saw what happened to my parents; I saw the doors kicked in when they came looking for my parents. Both my parents died—my father in prison in Paarl and my mother of a heart attack. My sister is mentally disabled because my mother was abused while pregnant. My brothers and sisters aren't educated, and they're suffering. I was shot many times, treated underground because we weren't allowed to go to the hospitals, so we tried to fix some of the wounds even though we weren't doctors. Because of this, I'm physically disabled. There were bullets we couldn't take out, clots, problems of blood circulation. I have an artificial leg.

There was a deal between the NP ["National Party"] and the ANC that if you allow us to run the country, we will seal the holes, we will help our people.[42] There was an argument between the ANC and the NP. Tutu said we went out of our way, the government should do something about us. Prosecutions won't take us anywhere. We'll help our people.

The TRC was very important to us because it was the beginning; that's why we supported it. The outcome was a problem. They should have given money to the comrades, not to build a stadium.[43] We don't feel we exist. Instead of a statue in Gugulethu, the money should have gone to the families. The TRC recommendations weren't followed because the president [Mbeki] doesn't care. I'm not going to say nice things because he's president. There was supposed to be money from the fund. Instead, money's going to the disaster fund. But what about us? My brothers and sisters aren't educated because the one who was responsible for our education was always in jail. Money should be provided for education, financial reparations, services. We

---

[41] Group Areas Act (Act No. 41 of 1950). Passed in 1950 by the South African Parliament, this Act reassigned sections of urban areas based on race, which led to the forcible removal of millions of non-whites from their homes and businesses in newly designated "white" areas.

[42] He refers to the political agreement between the ANC and the NP. The NP would relinquish much of its governing power to the ANC, but in exchange, the ANC would not pursue legal justice again NP party leaders and members.

[43] This is a reference to the government's investment in infrastructure for the 2010 World Cup, to be held in South Africa.

*were promised by Mbeki. It hurts and so you fight back, but it's
hard to fight the government. But we will. I don't feel a part of
this government. We feel this government is a threat to us. We
are trapped now. We feel as if we don't exist in this country. The
ANC for me is the only hope, and I feel trapped between the
past and present. We were always ANC and now are trapped
between the old and new government. I need help for the
future. Don't go around saying you're sorry. We need action.
Actions speak louder than words. We are described as moral
and spiritual. We don't need advice. We don't need to be told,
"Sorry, it was a mistake." We need the future.*

*They're paying millions a month to that Brazilian World
Cup coach, who will be a millionaire. He's going to go to his
damn country, and I was the one who fought through blood,
sweat, and tears for this democracy. And I still feel homeless
here. We who have been suffering so long get nothing.*

*Sometimes transformation without bloodshed is not
100%. Victims and perpetrators now don't really relate. They
feel they've done us a favor by letting us run the country; that we
didn't win it from them. That's why they don't respect us today.
Since 1994, we hear we were liberated. In 1998, there was worry
about problems, especially with land, so they are doing things to
show that we are nothing, even today. Transformation wasn't
done right. They were supposed to fight until someone gave
up. In other African countries they have no food, but they have
respect.*

Japhta Marawu
Khulumani Support Group
Cape Town, October 2006

C. The Amnesty Committee

Among the most controversial of the TRC's powers was its ability
to grant individual amnesty to those who fully disclosed the truth about
politically-motivated crimes. Amnesty was available to those who acted on
behalf of the former apartheid State as well as its political opponents.

The Amnesty Committee considered a number of factors to determine whether an act was associated with a political objective, including: (1) motive; (2) the context in which the act took place; (3) the objective of that act and whether it was directed at a political opponent or State property, or against private property or individuals; (4) whether the act was carried out as an order from or on behalf of an organization or movement of which the individual was a member or supporter; and (5) the relationship between the act and the political objective pursued, including whether there was proportionality between the act and the objective. An applicant seeking amnesty for gross violations of human rights was required to appear publicly and answer questions from the Committee, from legal counsel representing the victims and their families, and from victims themselves. However, no apology or sign of remorse was required in order to gain amnesty.

The Amnesty Committee was legalistic in its composition—in contrast to other TRC committees, all members of the Amnesty Committee were judges, advocates, or attorneys—and in its powers and procedures, such as its ability to subpoena witnesses and hold court-like hearings. Victims had the opportunity to challenge or cross-examine their purported victimizers, while perpetrators provided testimony with the support of lawyers. Those granted amnesty received protection from criminal and civil liability, and relieved the State of possible vicarious liability. The TRC operated on the premise that individuals who failed to seek amnesty or who did not qualify for amnesty would be recommended for prosecution, and confirmed this expectation in its Final Report: "Where amnesty has not been sought or has been denied, prosecution should be considered where evidence exists that an individual has committed a gross human rights violation."[44]

The TRC received over 7,000 applications for amnesty. In assessing these applications, the TRC determined that the apartheid State, and in particular its security apparatus and strategy formulation committees, were the primary perpetrators of gross human rights violations. However, the most senior members of the apartheid government refused to apply for amnesty and failed to acknowledge any wrongdoing, while continuing to express deep suspicion of the amnesty process. By the conclusion of the TRC, only 293 amnesty applications had come from members of the former government's security forces. Approximately 50% of these applications related to incidents that occurred between 1985 and 1989, and over 50% occurred in the Transvaal.[45] These applications related to 550 incidents comprising 1,583

---

[44] "Recommendations," *Truth and Reconciliation Commission of South Africa Report* (2003), Volume 5, Chapter 1, p. 309.
[45] "The Former South African Government and Its Security Forces," *Truth and Reconcili-*

separate acts, of which more than half were killings.[46] The vast majority of
these applications (256 or 87.4%) came from members of the SAP, of whom
229 were in the Security Branch at the time. Very few applications (31 or
10.6%) came from SADF members, evidencing their general reluctance to
participate in the amnesty process.[47] Of perpetrators for whom it was possible
to determine a rank, lower-ranking personnel committed 48% of the acts,
while 52% were committed by officers ranked lieutenant or above.[48] All
government-side applicants were male, and 86% were white.[49] Most of the
security force members who applied for amnesty did so without the support of
policymakers and politicians under whose orders they had operated.[50]

ANC-related amnesty applications were more abundant than those
of the government and far outnumber those from other parties opposing
apartheid, but relatively few applied overall. Such applications can be
divided into four broad categories: (1) applications from members of the
ANC leadership, the so-called "collective responsibility" applications; (2)
applications from MK operatives; (3) applications from Self-Defence Unit
("SDU") members; and (4) applications from civilians who were members
of, or who acted in the name of or in support of, the ANC. In total, 998
individual members or supporters of the ANC or related organizations applied
for amnesty for 1,025 incidents.[51] Nearly half occurred between 1990 and
1994, while another third occurred between 1985 and 1989, and over 60%
occurred in the Transvaal.[52] Many ANC members seeking amnesty expressed
a desire to participate in the TRC process and thereby support the new
democratic government's efforts towards social and political transformation
and reconciliation.[53] Some ANC party leaders, however, insisted members
had been fighting a just war against apartheid and therefore need not apply for

---

ation Commission of South Africa Report (2003), Volume 6, Section 3, Chapter 1, pp. 181,
188.
[46] *Ibid.*, p. 186. Of the 1,583 acts, 889 were categorized as killings, 143 as attempted killings,
98 as torture or assault, 83 as bombing or arson, and 80 as abduction.
[47] *Ibid.*, pp. 181-83.
[48] *Ibid.*, p. 188.
[49] *Ibid.*, p. 189.
[50] *Ibid.*, p. 183.
[51] "The ANC and Allied Organizations," *Truth and Reconciliation Commission of South
Africa Report* (2003), Volume 6, Section 3, Chapter 2, p. 265. Of the incidents, 42% were
attempted killings, 17% killings, and 12% attacks using explosives.
[52] *Ibid.*
[53] *Ibid.*, p. 266.

amnesty.[54]

Nevertheless, the ANC eventually adopted an official position that party leaders should accept full political and moral responsibility for the actions of their members. A number of National Executive Committee members did then submit collective amnesty applications, framed as "Declarations of Responsibility." The Declaration applicants did not specify particular acts but rather attempted to take collective responsibility for gross human rights violations committed by MK and SDU operatives. Amnesties were initially granted for these collective declarations but subsequently overturned by the Constitutional Court. Upon reconsideration before the Committee, amnesty was refused on the grounds that these applications failed to comply with the requirement to specify particular acts, omissions, or offences committed by the individual applicant.[55]

From the outset, the IFP also expressed reservations about and even hostility toward the TRC.[56] IFP President Mangosuthu Buthelezi maintained that IFP members who carried out illegal activities had acted on their own initiative in response to the violence of the time.[57] Thus, although the IFP appeared before the Commission, it did not cooperate with the Amnesty Committee or participate in the amnesty process. As a result, without the support of the party to vouch for the political motives of their actions, only 109 applications were received from IFP members and supporters for incidents that occurred between 1987 and 1994.[58] These applications came primarily from military operatives. The Committee did not receive applications from any high-ranking members of the national or provincial political leadership of the IFP.[59] Some of the applicants were in the service of SAP or SADF at the time of the offences and alleged, along with other SADF-trained applicants, that these organizations had sponsored or colluded in the atrocities. Many IFP applicants had already been convicted of the offences for which they sought amnesty or had been implicated and anticipated prosecution.[60] The Committee granted amnesty to 60 IFP applicants (57%) and refused amnesty to 40 (38%), with the remainder being either reclassified as non-IFP applicants or denied amnesty

---

[54] *Ibid.*

[55] *Ibid.*, pp. 271-72.

[56] "The Inkatha Freedom Party," *Truth and Reconciliation Commission of South Africa Report* (2003), Volume 6, Section 3, Chapter 3, p. 338.

[57] *Ibid.*, p. 342.

[58] *Ibid.*, pp. 340-41.

[59] *Ibid.*, p. 346.

[60] *Ibid.*, p. 340.

for certain incidents while receiving it for others.[61]

Members and supporters of the PAC and the APLA applied for amnesty for a range of offences, including violations in PAC camps, attacks on security forces, attacks on white farmers and civilians, armed robberies, and sabotage operations.[62] In total, 138 applicants, all male, applied for a total of 204 violations, with the majority concentrated in the Western Cape between 1990 and 1994 and committed by APLA operatives.[63] The Committee granted amnesty for 155 of those 204 acts, or 76%.[64]

The Amnesty Committee also received 107 applications from members of right-wing groups, which it defined as groups, often emerging from conservative Afrikaner circles, organized "to campaign for self-determination" and "mobilized against the democratic changes sweeping South Africa in the early 1990s."[65] The Committee found a spike in violence by these groups as elections approached in 1994, with the majority of the violations occurring in the former Orange Free State and Transvaal.[66] Nearly 70% of right-wing applicants were granted amnesty for acts including attacks on individuals, possession of arms, explosives, and ammunition, sabotage of the transitional process, and sabotage of the electoral process.[67]

By the time the Amnesty Committee completed its work in June 2001, it had granted amnesty to 1,160 of 7,094 applicants, slightly more than 15% of those who had applied.[68] This left thousands of individuals who sought amnesty without any shield from prosecution, in addition to the unknown number of perpetrators who never sought amnesty before the TRC. The narratives that follow capture the complex interplay between truth-telling, reparations, amnesty, prosecution, and reconciliation that for many characterizes the relationship between the TRC process and the question of further prosecution.

---

[61] *Ibid.*, p. 345.

[62] "The Pan Africanist Congress," *Truth and Reconciliation Commission of South Africa Report* (2003), Volume 6, Section 3, Chapter 4, p. 375.

[63] *Ibid.*, pp. 375-76.

[64] *Ibid.*, p. 375.

[65] "Right-Wing Groups," *Truth and Reconciliation Commission of South Africa Report* (2003), Volume 6, Section 3, Chapter 6, pp. 444, 452.

[66] *Ibid.*, p. 452.

[67] *Ibid.*, pp. 452-53.

[68] Amnesty International, *Truth and Justice: Unfinished Business in South Africa* (2003), http://web.amnesty.org.

During apartheid, from 1976 onward especially, our houses and shops were burned down, people drank fish oil because they had to, they drank powdered milk because we didn't have anything [because of the consumer boycott]. And the ANC was punishing people who broke the boycott. I was living in Langa in 1976. I was 24 and had a citizen pass from Ciskei but no permit to be in Cape Town. I was arrested and tortured for not having a pass. The policemen took us to Pollsmoor for three days. In 1986, I was tortured in KTC,[69] and they took me to Somerset Hospital. I was in the hospital for a month because of the tear gas, and I was pregnant at the time. I had a child, who's now 22 years old. My knees still hurt because of the torture. My brother was there in the house in KTC too and was tortured also. I didn't go to the TRC because I didn't know about it. We started Khulumani in Woodstock at the Trauma Centre in 1995. My family was in the ANC, and I'm still a member.

I want them to be prosecuted—de Klerk, the other leaders who were suggesting to them what to do. It was Mr. Barnard who tortured me, but he's dead now. Other black people who supported that government should be prosecuted too.

I didn't approve of the idea of amnesty. It did nothing for us. We got nothing. To have people hear my story is important to me, but I need reparations too. I think we got more truth at the TRC. But the truth is that most people were killed. Amnesty was not important because it was not going to change the fact that people had already been killed. It was not going to change anything. Many people I know now testified at the TRC, but I only heard about it after the doors were closed. I found out later that they had told stories. I don't know why people weren't speaking about it at the time. I had a Hi-Fi [radio] but no TV, no way to hear about the hearings. I felt bad that I hadn't known about the TRC.

Today there is nothing. We have no voice. I am not working. That's something I blame on apartheid. My daughter can't continue with her studies after matric because I can't afford the study fees. That's from apartheid. The government should

---

[69] KTC was a squatter camp created in 1975 following the Group Areas Act.

*help us to help our children. But our government has fallen
asleep. Mbeki's on cloud nine, dreaming, and our children go to
work as domestic workers. Mbeki doesn't want to help. We've
been knocking on doors, but he didn't help. The only thing we
need is help. They must give us our reparations. Enough is
enough.*

Nomonde Mbangamganthi
Khulumani Support Group
Cape Town, October 2006

*There is the view that people have been granted amnesty
and are still living lives of luxury while victims and their families
are still suffering and living lives of poverty. People ask, "Where
is the justice?" There wasn't anything punitive, and obviously
amnesty isn't about punishment. . . .*

*I think that if we go back to the objective of the TRC
itself and forget about amnesty, it is about being able to draw
the picture for people, to say, "This is what happened." I think
that in the process of truth and reconciliation, the objective is
not to start pointing out individuals and pursuing them. There
wouldn't have been anyone left to run the country after that. In
some way or another everyone would have had some kind of
finger pointing or accusations hurled at them.*

*In the process of achieving the truth we are saying we
want full disclosure; but the outcome was that amnesty was
granted, and in a sense, it was teaching people that we need
to forgive others because they are telling the truth. The TRC
achieved that form of reconciliation. I think that is one of the
biggest feathers in our cap, because we got through the first
elections and our second elections and there wasn't violence.*

*That's not to say that people are all happy. Of course I
think our biggest failure has been the reparations fund. People
are still sitting waiting for payments, and lots of victims and
families of victims still feel aggrieved; they feel that justice has
not been done. But I think that is a natural feeling. You are*

never going to get 100% positive responses after what South Africa has been through.

Anonymous
Instructor of Law
Durban, January 2007

V. THE UNFINISHED BUSINESS OF THE TRC

Many describe the TRC as a miracle of transitional justice and commend its accomplishments. It gathered and exposed an enormous amount of information about South Africa's apartheid era. Victims who had long been dispossessed and disempowered played essential roles in telling their national history. The public continues to return to the TRC and its reports, drawing on its extensive resources, scrutinizing its limitations and failings, and attempting to tackle the questions left unanswered. Measured by this continuous engagement with its legacy, the TRC was a successful enterprise.

However, this ongoing engagement with the TRC results, in part, from lingering ambiguities and persistent frustrations over the adequacy of the process. Its Final Report was intended to initiate a national discussion and set policy directives related not only to national healing, social and economic transformation, and reparations, but also to the pursuit of justice against apartheid-era perpetrators. Former TRC Commissioner and Advocate Dumisa Ntsebeza observes that: "The TRC never really dealt with the issues between the beneficiaries and victims of economic apartheid. How can you deal with the issues of apartheid without looking at the entire structure of the system, in every area?"[70] Despite the work of the TRC, the common dream of a better future has diminished for many South Africans. The TRC was less than successful in addressing structural inequalities and facilitating broad discussions about social justice. Many South Africans still live in conditions that are strikingly similar to those of the apartheid era, and the reparations that have been distributed are widely perceived as inadequate. Economic inequalities in South Africa are among the worst in the world. HIV/AIDS continues to ravage the country and violent crime threatens South Africans of all races. Thus, the disparity between hopes for reconciliation and the lack of transformation persists in the midst of other urgent social problems.

---

[70] International Human Rights Clinic Interview with Dumisa Ntsebeza, Former TRC Commissioner, Advocate, Cape Town, South Africa, Oct. 2006.

South Africans' widespread understanding was that prosecutions would follow and build upon the work of the TRC, and most imagined that these prosecutions would begin immediately. Amidst everyday demands and against the background of high expectations among the general population, the paucity of prosecutions represents a major component of the TRC's incomplete legacy. Striking an appropriate balance between continuing to pursue apartheid-era perpetrators and tackling other immediate needs remains one of South Africa's most intricate challenges. As the following narratives demonstrate, victims are themselves divided about whether amnesty was a necessary or acceptable compromise, whether they most desire prosecutions or reparations, whether forgiveness and reconciliation are possible, and what steps might best continue the process of transformation initiated by the TRC.

> *I'm from the outer province in the Eastern Cape. In June 1991, I was shot with buckshot in both legs while leading a march as an ANC Youth League leader with the UDF ["United Democratic Front"]. We were marching to Queenstown, to the Ciskei government. When we were coming back to Ciskei, there was a police station and teaching college. The police came with buses, some in the station, and they started shooting. There were no warnings. I was in front. They were always harassing me because I was too [politically] active in the area. I started running, then fell. Some comrades went to the police, got me, and took me to the hospital. The police and soldiers were there, stopping people from seeing me because I was a leader and they might have sneaked in and taken me away.*
>
> *I stayed in the hospital about two weeks, and [the police] were always watching me. After that they took me to the hospital in East London. The specialist there said I'd live 50 years, so they discharged me to the police to wait for court. They gave me a court date, but I was harassed all the time, including while I was in the house, even at night. I was with my mother, wife, children. They started coming to the house every night. On September 3, 1991, I went to court, and they dismissed the case. They were always surveilling me, always watching me . . . .*
>
> *I did participate in the TRC. It was good. I felt comfort that I told the story, and they accepted it, although they didn't do what they should have done. They gave me reparations of 5,000 rand and 30,000 rand later, but I too am complaining. I got a*

letter from Mandela saying they would help with education and work. The house needs help; I have health problems, but when Mbeki came in, he said there would be a once-off payment. It seems like the TRC was a joke. There were people disabled, dead, and what the president did to us is not something we should forget.

I do not feel that the soldiers who shot me should be prosecuted. No. We have [to] forget, to give the country a chance to move forward to democracy. If the families were okay with amnesty, if the families participated [at the TRC] and accepted amnesty, then it was okay. It might be fair to have amnesty, but there are others who didn't come forward to tell the truth, who stayed quiet behind closed doors. The leaders of the past government should have come forward, and they didn't. But I still think about others behind closed doors, like Botha. Why are they not coming forward for the nation to see? All those who led should come forward and tell their stories. The big leaders of the government—the Minister of Justice, the President, Botha, Vlok—those under them were instructed to do it. They were giving instructions. That's what we want everyone to know about. We want to know about the commands. The government now is not doing what they said they should. Now, it seems as if the president doesn't want to listen to anyone.

I don't blame the TRC. The TRC Commissioners support us. I blame the government. The government said that the struggle was not for payment, that they would give 30,000 rand, and that [this amount] was not negotiable. But the fact that the president doesn't want to listen is the most frustrating.

Nyanisile Rholihlahla
Khulumani Support Group
Cape Town, October 2006

I'm 33 years old, from the Eastern Cape, came to Cape Town when I was ten years old in 1984. I remember people talking about the forced removals, KTC, and I was living with my aunt and uncle. My parents were still in the Eastern Cape. I

*remember in Standard Two, the Hippos[71] coming through. We
had to repeat a year of school because the government closed
the schools in June because the students were protesting. It was
more the high school students, especially in Gugulethu.*

*In 1993, I was finishing matric. In 1994, I was doing a
bridging course. I remember it was the first year we got IDs, and
I remember elections were going on. I knew there was a TRC,
I knew about it—according to Dumisa's book[72] and my idea, it
was the apartheid regime under pressure to put up a structure.
There were negotiations taking place. Why did the government
decide to destroy all those documents? They wanted to forget
the past. They didn't want black people to know what happened.
Why wasn't there more time? Why didn't people know more?*

*There was a scandal in the Eastern Cape when five
children were killed at a PAC member's house in Umtata by
the death squads and that was the same year that de Klerk got
the Nobel Prize. They just covered up. So, most things were
happening in the homelands, and people didn't know about it.
You didn't know the politics somewhere else. There are lots of
stories that were told, and it's impossible for them to find out
everything.*

*The TRC was just window dressing; deep down, the
whites just wanted to satisfy Mandela, but there wasn't really
any reconciliation. [Those who received amnesty] should die
and rot in hell. It was a big mistake to give amnesty. It didn't
help to get more truth. These people here are still suffering, and
they've gotten nothing. Even if reparations had all worked, the
perpetrators should still have gone to jail. It's never too late for
prosecutions. Botha, Vlok, all of them.[73] I'd love to see them
shrinking in hell. Washing the feet[74]—that was just an act
because he's going to jail. They always lie.*

The IFP was used by the apartheid government because

---

[71] Hippos were armored vehicles used by the South African security forces.

[72] Dumisa Ntsebeza, along with Terry Bell, co-authored *Unfinished Business: South Africa,
Apartheid, and Truth* (London: Verso, 2003).

[73] P.W. Botha was the former South African president, predecessor to F.W. de Klerk, and a
notoriously staunch proponent of apartheid. See Chapter Four for a more thorough discussion of Adriaan Vlok's role in the apartheid state.

[74] Gert Coetzee and Liezel de Lange, "Why Vlok Washed Chikane's Feet," News 24, Aug. 27,
2006, http://www.news24.com/News24/South_Africa/Politics/0,,2-7-12_1989193,00.html.

*the Inkatha members were deployed all over Cape Town because
they were against school boycotts. They would beat kids if they
found them in the house when they were supposed [to be] in
school. They should die a slow painful death too. Apologies
aren't enough. Even if Vlok comes and washes our feet, it doesn't
change what they did. To their eyes, we looked like animals.
The black government is still window dressing. No matter where
you go, there are still white faces everywhere. Even today, we
can't get jobs because if you have a name they can't pronounce,
they just won't hire you. They'll call you in and then look at
your name and if it's African, they'll just not take you.*

F.G.
Khulumani Support Group
Cape Town, October 2006

REFLECTION

"I know they talk about reconciliation at a national level. But with me, as a person, as someone who's gone through the pain, I feel like I also need revenge."

Nombuyiselo Mhlauli, Cradock Four Widow
Cape Town, March 2008

I think that the TRC process, for me, was quite good. It helped me a lot because we were able to go there and tell our stories about the suffering we have gone through over the years. So it was a good opportunity for us to let the people know how we felt over the years, because we never had an opportunity to express our own views. Always people talked on behalf of us on various platforms, without really coming to us and asking, "What do you feel about the whole thing?" So that space was open for us at the TRC.

Before going to the TRC, we didn't have any expectations around getting any financial gain out of the whole thing. But when we went before the TRC, some questions were thrown to us, to say, "What is it that you'd like to get after the TRC?" And we mentioned a number of things, like education for the children; others [said] accommodation, things like that. As time went by, our expectations were raised to a certain level by saying you do have a right at the end of the day to launch a legal suit against the perpetrators. And we thought, okay, that will be fine, we will be quite happy to do that. As time went by we then again [were told] no, you do not have a right [to bring suit]. We don't know what this legal document is that prevented us from doing that. But anyway the perpetrators themselves, the killers, most of them didn't go before the TRC. Most of them didn't go before the Amnesty Committee, and those who went before the Amnesty Committee did not tell the full story so that we could get the answers for our questions.

[When I appeared before the TRC] I was really keen to know who exactly killed my husband. Who stabbed him? Forty-six wounds all over his body. Forty-six. Different sizes of knives were used to stab him. So I needed to know exactly who did that. And I wanted to be taken to the scene where this happened. In fact, we did make a request that we really want to be taken to that scene, so that [we could] know exactly where they were killed. It never happened. So we still remained with those questions. Where were they actually killed? And who were the actual people who were in on the act? Those questions were never answered, up to today. We wanted them [the perpetrators] to come to us so that we could sit and talk to them and [hear them] answer whatever we wanted to ask from them. Because we still had questions to throw to them ourselves. That never happened. So we moved on, in a way.

I'm interested in the full story. But on top of the story they should also get a bit of a punishment. I mean now it's long overdue, and it looks like, if ever they do come now, I would say they were not really interested in coming forward. That's why I'm saying even if they do come, I still feel like they should get their punishment, they should also pay the price. I never had the wish that these people should just talk and talk and leave [with] nothing happening to them, whilst we've suffered so much and people were murdered so brutally. We wanted them to pay the price as well. Well, that never happened. It's a long time ago. It's almost twenty years now. But up until now nobody has ever even attempted to say, "Okay, now I want to come forward to you guys and tell you exactly what has happened." So we are still sitting with that deep-seated bitterness or anger with us.

I don't know what to say, you know. I really don't know what to say. But my wish is that even if they are 80 or 70 years old, they should still get their own punishment in terms of what they've done. I know they are saying that it was because of the laws of that time, but of course, yes, they've committed a crime that they should pay for. That's my personal view; if they can go before the court of law, then the law decides what is . . . the sentence. But I would be very much comfortable with giving them a life sentence so that their families experience exactly what we've experienced over the years.

We depended on our own families and other people who could come and support [us], and we've never been taken through the whole pain so that [we] can get to terms with it. Because it's so difficult to get to terms with it. We keep on reflecting back, and it really emotionally affects me. For instance, if I have some challenges, I keep thinking back. It can't go away completely. I just can't take it out of my mind.

I think my interest . . . would be that these guys are taken back to court to be prosecuted. I know that it will never bring the life back, [but] prosecutions would be my number one [priority]. I don't know whether I'm too negative. I still have that—I still need the revenge. So that they can feel exactly the pain. I want their families to experience exactly what we experienced, because it looks like they don't understand exactly. [To them] it's something that has happened; it's over, it's past. If ever they can be prosecuted, prosecutions would be the number one [priority] to me. Then reparations can follow, because I've already gone so long without reparations, so I don't think they will ever change my life as such. If I were to say, "Okay, I just need reparations now without them being prosecuted," I wouldn't be doing justice to myself. I know that what I want is to see them going through the same things, the pain that we've gone through. If they give me money only, then they won't go through the same pain. They can always work for their money.

I know people don't want to talk about revenge. It's there. I know that we've been told that we should reconcile, we should build a nation together. It's true we have to do that. But, within me, I still have that. I honestly still [do]. I'm telling you what I feel as a person now, not as a nation. I know they talk about reconciliation at a national level. But with me, as a person, as someone who's gone through the pain, I feel like I also need revenge. I don't know which other word, which lighter word I can use.

I don't think [the politicians] are taking us seriously. They don't. Why I'm saying that? There are various things that should have been implemented by the government to show that they really care about our victims. I'll make an example about people who lost their children in the battlefield, children who died inside the country as well, including our husbands. Others just disappeared, they're not known where they are, and parents kept on requesting, "If we can only get the remains of our children." And nothing was done about that.

I was personally working [with the] South African Heritage Resources Agency. I would meet with other victims because my area of work was to interact with the victims to construct or erect some commemorative structures. People were not really happy about that. They'd say, "What I'm interested in is my child. I'm interested in the remains of my child." At that time there was nothing we could do beyond our mandate. We had to go to the government itself to say people are making these requests. The former Minister of Justice, I don't want to mention her name, just said, "Where is the government going to get money from to bring back all those remains?" It hurt me so much. I'm facing these people, I don't have an answer to them, and the fact [was] they requested something that was very important.

In our country, we are busy with Freedom Park.[75] But I don't know whether it's really going to be a structure that will heal the wounds of the people. Because I know that the grave of my son is not there, or the grave of my husband is not there. Is it really going to make an impact within me? Is

---

[75] Freedom Park is a memorial and museum outside Pretoria meant to reflect South Africa's history and its political, social, and economic struggles. For more information, see http://www.southafrica.info/about/history/freedompark.htm.

it going to heal me? Is it going to make me feel good about it? I don't know whether [it will].

So that's why I'm saying I don't think they've made a full effort. I know others might be very angry about what I'm saying, but again I'm saying it's my personal feeling. There's a tendency of thinking that some victims are victims at higher levels than the others, even though the pain is the same. We've all lost lives; we lost our people; we lost our soldiers. I just want to make an emphasis that death is death, at the end of the day. We cannot grade death, saying the death of this one is better than the death of the other one, because the pain is the same.

I must be honest with you now. Immediately after the incident [of my husband's murder], I was so bitter, very angry. But I think my own thinking and perceptions were sort of—I don't want to say manipulated—but things happened that made me accept certain things even though within me I thought, [I do not feel comfortable]. I don't know how to put it. Like for instance, when Madiba [Mandela] said, "You must forgive and forget," I thought to myself, how do I forgive and forget when my husband has been killed so brutally? When my husband has been buried without his hand? When his face has been [disfigured], they threw acid over his face? I said to myself, dear me, how do I forget all those things? It's difficult for me to forget those things. And in the process of not forgetting those things, I become so angry. I don't want to forgive fully. I know that.

My own daughter said, before the TRC, "We are prepared to forgive, but we want to know who is it, exactly." Well, that's the view of the country, that's the view of my daughter. And I thought, alright, let me not be so hard to myself, let me accept this as the country is seeking forgiveness. But when you talk [about] the country, it's a different thing at a different level. When you bring it closer to you, you might feel differently from that view. We were saying, oh dear me, [Mandela] is saying you must forgive and forget. Of course, yes, Mandela spent so many years in jail, but he's happy to be alive. The others are not alive.

One other thing that I think hurt us so much, or hurt me so much, is when people are saying, "When people joined the struggle, they didn't join the struggle in order to get some benefits or gain or money." You know, that was very painful because most of them, in a way, [have received a form of reparations] because they are serving in government, they are paid well, they've got good jobs. Whereas others don't have good jobs. Like the four of us [Cradock Four widows], we've been going through thick and thin—lose jobs, be at home, unemployed, things like that—and nobody ever said, "Let me come closer to those [women]. How are things with you?" Those who came closer, they would come in close to us because they wanted to benefit themselves, not us.

Of course [talking about the past] does bring back the pain. But if people talk, say for instance [when] the victims themselves are together, we tend to listen to someone else's story and think, "Oh dear me. I thought that my story was the worst. But this one is worse than mine." So that, in a way, heals you. In a way. In many instances, when people are organized together, they are able to think and focus and identify exactly what it is that they would like to see happening.

It will be good to bring the whole thing on track again, so that they [the government] start thinking about it. There are so many people. Maybe they don't realize that people are so bitter because they don't come closer to the people and understand exactly the feelings of people. Once the information is gathered and brought back to them, maybe they will start sitting down and thinking, "Dear me, we haven't done any justice to these people."

Reflection

"A process of bringing together victims and offenders is very important."

Paddy Kearney, Former Head of the Diakonia Council of Churches, Consultant
Durban, January 2007

The TRC was effective in giving some people the opportunity to tell their stories. Our [Diakonia Council of Churches] Community Resource Centres worked with the TRC. They encouraged people to tell their stories, they helped the victims to tell them, and some of those people were invited to tell their stories in TRC public hearings. I think the importance of storytelling is prime: people really value telling their story in a formal process, being taken seriously and listened to.

The TRC was successful in revealing the truth, but it did little on reconciliation. There was a lot of frustration because wounds had been opened up by telling stories and then there was no follow-up in terms of reconciliation. We needed another structure or process, so people didn't just tell stories and go home. There needed to be a process of bringing them together with perpetrators—going into in-depth processes of reconciliation, of healing. There was plenty of scope for . . . people to be trained in [addressing] stress and trauma. It is going on now with Diakonia and Father Michael Lapsley's organization [Institute for Healing of Memories][76] and a number of other initiatives, but much more extensive work of this kind is needed. This should have happened parallel to the hearings. A huge task of healing needed to be done and still needs to be done. It needed skilled people—the churches could have played a role—but beyond this too, there needed to be resources. By the time the TRC came to the churches and said your role is reconciliation, it was very late in the process, and no government resources were made available to the churches as had been the case for the TRC.

If you compare the swiftness of amnesty with the slowness of reparation, the compensation given by government, which was actually very little, came years later for the victims. That was in a way the worst thing about the reparations: too little and too late, and not done in a way that recognized that not only individuals but also whole communities suffered. I am not sure it was helpful to give a family ZAR 30,000. What might have been more effective

---

[76] For more information, see http://www.healingofmemories.co.za/.

was perhaps to build a new school, a new hospital which would benefit a whole community, recognizing that in some places everyone had suffered.

Dr. Deon Snyman is a Dutch Reformed Church minister in the Cape who has set up a Restitution Trust and is working . . . to get white people to see that they have benefited from apartheid. This sort of work is one model that could be looked at. It is not easy work, but the Restitution Trust has set up a number of discussion groups, which are looking at various ways in which restitution can be made. They have had people coming forward to say, "You can have my farm to promote community development," and people have also paid in sums of money. The Restitution Trust encourages people to meet others across the racial barriers and share their skills. People from the business community could share their skills with communities which are just starting their own small businesses. The scale of this kind of work should be greatly increased. Government money could be put in to promote this kind of work.

A post-amnesty process is necessary to show perpetrators that they can't go skipping down the road with their amnesty. I agree [that amnesty was a necessary political compromise], but there should be an adjunct to it, saying that there is something else that the perpetrators need to do; to go through a process of repentance. There should have been a mechanism to encourage them to repent and to propose ways in which that repentance could be shown. There was a lot of questioning whether there was any repentance involved in many of the cases where people were given amnesty.

I wonder whether the threat of prosecution may be useful. . . . The situation can't just be left as it is now. Perhaps it needs elements of the healing process as well as those of a prosecutorial process. At the moment we are doing nothing. I think there needs to be some process, some formal legal process that goes to people who didn't apply for amnesty, that tells them what you have done is a major problem. We need to think through this very carefully. You cannot leave these people out. You must embarrass them and put some options to them. . . . It must be something serious, some procedure, engaging with a judge. . . . It must be jointly facilitated by NGOs and government. You could have the psychologists there. It can't be too easy, so [that] people just laugh it off. There must be serious consequences, and the whole process must be serious. Will perpetrators who did not apply for amnesty take this additional process seriously if they are not arrested, charged, and brought to court? I doubt it.

CHAPTER 3

Prosecutorial Powers in South Africa

[Prosecutions of apartheid-era human rights offenders who were not granted amnesty] will be part and parcel of what the National Prosecuting Authority will be doing henceforth. [It is] a legacy of what we live with as South Africans and as a country.

Fatima Chohan-Kota, Chairperson,
Parliamentary Committee on Justice and Constitutional Development
January 2006[77]

They should have had a policy in place saying that for those who don't apply for amnesty, this is what is going to happen to you: vigorous prosecution.

Robin Palmer, Professor of Law
Durban, January 2007

I. INTRODUCTION

In South Africa, as in many countries, the question of who is

---

[77] Shaun Benton, "Policy on Prosecution of Apartheid-era Human Rights Offenders Unveiled," Bua News Online, Jan. 17, 2006, http://www.buanews.gov.za/view.php?ID=0601180 8151002&coll=buanew06.

prosecuted, and for what crimes, is answered by prosecutors acting for the State. Since the end of apartheid, South Africa's NPA has exercised great discretionary powers in deciding when and whether to bring cases against perpetrators of gross human rights violations.

This chapter explores the role of prosecutorial discretion and examines the amended guidelines promulgated by the NPA in late 2005, and well as a constitutional challenge to those guidelines. Several key trends emerge, each with a profound impact on the nature, and dearth, of apartheid-era prosecutions. First, the issue of how much discretion the NPA should exercise in apartheid-era cases has received much less attention than the issue of how the TRC would be structured and its mandate implemented. While the creation of the TRC was prominently debated, aside from concerned members of civil society relatively little public energy has been devoted to the question of how the NPA manages apartheid-era cases. Second, as a result of this first trend, the bureaucracy of the government and the NPA itself have largely defined its prosecutorial powers, without input from victims and without any sustained national-level discussion. Third, as a consequence of these first two trends, although the NPA's prosecutions policy with regard to apartheid-era crimes has evolved over the years, it has also drifted. A lack of public consultation and waning political will to bring cases has led to indecision and inaction by the NPA. The constitutional challenge to the guidelines can be understood as a direct response to these trends. It represents an effort by victims to publicly engage with the prosecutions question and have their voices heard in the policy-making process, in order to shape the discretionary powers of the NPA with respect to apartheid-era cases.

II. Background

A. The NPA

The NPA was established in the 1996 Constitution as South Africa's single prosecuting authority, with "the power to institute criminal proceedings on behalf of the state, and to carry out any necessary functions incidental to instituting criminal proceedings."[78] The Constitution created the office of the National Director of Public Prosecutions ("NDPP") with the authority to determine prosecutions policy for the country, in consultation with relevant

---

[78] Constitution of the Republic of South Africa (Act No. 108 of 1996), art. 179(2).

Cabinet members and the Directors of Public Prosecutions.[79] The NDPP
was also empowered to review a decision to prosecute (or not to prosecute)
after taking representations from the accused, the complainant, and any
other relevant parties.[80] Accordingly, the Constitution granted considerable
discretion to the NDPP to determine whether to pursue prosecutions or
plea arrangements in criminal cases, and charged the NPA with carrying
out its work "without fear, favour, or prejudice."[81] The Constitutional Court
subsequently indicated that the NPA is bound to prosecute when there is a
prima facie case and a "reasonable and probable cause for prosecution."[82] The
Court further confirmed, in *State v. Basson*, that the NPA, as a representative
of the community, is required to prosecute crimes of the apartheid era:
"international law obliged the State to punish crimes against humanity and war
crimes. It is also clear that the practice of apartheid constituted crimes against
humanity and some of the practices of the apartheid government constituted
war crimes."[83]

South African prosecutors have always had the ability to negotiate
plea bargains and to ask judges to grant immunity in exchange for self-
incriminating testimony.[84] The law has also required that prosecutors give
"due regard" to the "interests of the community" when making plea bargains.[85]
Prior to 1996, provincial attorneys-general also had substantial independence
from political influence.[86] The establishment of the NPA in 1996 strengthened
central government control over prosecutions.[87] The first post-apartheid
prosecutions policy was presented to parliament in 1999, and was intended
to enhance public confidence in the legal system.[88] The policy outlined the
manner in which prosecutors should exercise their discretion at all stages
in the criminal justice process, from deciding whether to pursue a case to
deciding whether to accept a plea agreement, and required prosecutors to

---

[79] *Ibid.*, art. 179(5).
[80] *Ibid.*
[81] *Ibid.*, art. 179(4).
[82] *Beckenshroter v. Rottcher and Theunissen*, 1955(1) SA 129 (AD), para. 137.
[83] *State v. Basson*, 2005 (1) SA 171 (Const. Ct.), para. 37.
[84] Lovell Fernandez, "Post-TRC Prosecutions in South Africa," *Justice in Transition Prosecution and Amnesty in Germany and South Africa* (Gerhard Werle ed., 2006), pp. 68–70.
[85] Criminal Procedure Act (Act. No. 51 of 1977) Section 105A.
[86] Martin Schönteich, Institute for Security Studies, *Lawyers for the People: The South African Prosecution Service* (2001), http://www.iss.co.za/index.php?link_id=24&slink_id=466&link_type=12&slink_type=12&tmpl_id=3.
[87] *Ibid.*
[88] *Ibid.*

consider the public interest when selecting whom to prosecute.[89]

That same year, a unit within the NPA was established to build upon the TRC process by determining which individuals not granted amnesty would be prosecuted for their acts, and then pursuing such cases.[90] Initially known as the Special National Projects Unit, it was restructured and renamed the Priority Crimes Litigation Unit (PCLU) in 2003.[91]

> *Like others, I struggled with the question of amnesty at first. Some commissioners hadn't followed the preparation for the Truth and Reconciliation Commission Act and were shocked to find out that amnesty would be a part of the work. But I gradually came to realize that amnesty was necessary, that without it, we would not have peaceful elections. We hoped that, for the sake of truth, amnesty would be useful and that reparations would somehow make up for the incapacity to prosecute [those who qualified for amnesty]. Amnesty was the price we paid for peace, and full disclosure was the price we [demanded] for amnesty.*
>
> *We always understood that there would be prosecutions—that those who did not seek amnesty would be prosecuted. It was the logical outcome. Naming and shaming is not enough; people should not be able to get off scot-free. Justice means paying a penalty to society for infringement or abuse; a loss of liberty is the one most victims expect. A prison sentence is appropriate for gross crimes or perhaps people could pay fines which go back into society. Justice means if you committed an offence you do something to make up for it—you could say a sense of putting something right.*
>
> *The lack of prosecutions has been a real problem and has really devalued the work of the Truth Commission. It was a mistake that all the prosecutions [during the period of the TRC] were held up every time there was an amnesty application. That made it difficult to move anything forward, and it prevented the prosecutions from having the same amount of power. On the other hand, there were cases with an enormous amount of*

---

[89] *Ibid.*
[90] Jeremy Sarkin, *Carrots and Sticks: The TRC and the South African Amnesty Process* (New York: Intersentia, 2004), p. 375.
[91] *Ibid.*

*evidence, but prosecutors were not able to secure convictions.
In those cases, it was better to go the amnesty route and hope
reparations would make up for the absence of the capacity to
prosecute. Time makes prosecutions less and less a possibility,
and not just because of prescription.[92] Evidence is harder to get.
Presumably, that's what's holding up the NPA. But I am sure
there must be enough evidence; we submitted the information
we had to the prosecutors. I can't help feeling that there's a lack
of will and lack of resources. We are told that the NPA has cases
in the pipeline, but it has been twelve years. The focus now
should be (a) can you get a conviction, and (b) will it bring out
more information than we had before? Government's emphasis
is on the present, not on the past. It has a lot of problems now.*

Mary Burton
Former TRC Commissioner, Activist
Cape Town, October 2006

B. The NPA's Post-TRC Mandate

On March 21, 2003, the TRC concluded a lengthy and difficult process with the release of the last two volumes of the Final Report, which included a comprehensive list of over 1,100 individuals granted amnesty. In a speech to Parliament on April 15, 2003, then-President Thabo Mbeki stated:

Government is of the firm conviction that we cannot resolve
this matter by setting up yet another amnesty process, which
in effect would mean suspending constitutional rights of
those who were at the receiving end of gross human rights
violations. We have therefore left this matter in the hands
of the National Directorate of Public Prosecutions, for it to
pursue any cases that, as is normal practice, it believes deserve
prosecution and can be prosecuted. This work is continuing.
However, as part of this process and in the national interest,
the National Directorate of Public Prosecutions, working with
our intelligence agencies, will leave its doors open for those

---

[92] The legal definition of "prescription" is the limitation of time beyond which a crime is no longer eligible for prosecution.

who are prepared to divulge information at their disposal and to cooperate in unearthing the truth, for them to enter into arrangements that are standard in the normal execution of justice, and which are accommodated in our legislation.[93]

President Mbeki's speech conveyed two important messages about the transition from the granting of amnesty by the TRC to the pursuit of prosecutions by the NPA. It reminded the country of the NPA's mandate to prosecute apartheid-era cases while, at the same time, alluding to the prosecutorial discretion routinely exercised in deciding whether to pursue a particular case or negotiate a plea agreement with accused perpetrators.[94] In this instance, such discretion meant that the NDPP would have the legal authority to treat apartheid-era cases in the same manner as other criminal cases, pursuing those that the NPA determined deserved prosecution and had a reasonable chance of success, or entering into plea agreements where appropriate.

President Mbeki did not make clear, however, why such critical and politically-sensitive cases, emanating from the work of the TRC, should be handled with procedures that are "standard in the normal execution of justice." His comments were open to widely divergent interpretations. They could be read to indicate that apartheid-era cases might lose priority among the NPA's other pressing concerns, or conversely to emphasize that rather than allowing apartheid-related cases to stagnate, the NPA should treat them with the same urgency and seriousness as present-day crime. President Mbeki's comments may have been a public foreshadowing of subsequent decisions to pursue only a limited number of prosecutions, or may simply have been intended to remind perpetrators that the option remained to come forward as State's witnesses, even in apartheid-era cases, as is standard procedure in other criminal prosecutions.

The debate over the true meaning of President Mbeki's comments intensified in reaction to the NPA's amended prosecutions policy. The NPA already had an established prosecutions policy in place when tasked with

---

[93] President Thabo Mbeki, "Statement to the National Houses of Parliament and the Nation, at the Tabling of the Report of the Truth and Reconciliation Commission," April 15, 2003, http://www.anc.org.za/ancdocs/history/mbeki/2003/tm0415.html.

[94] Prosecutorial discretion is a standard power granted to prosecutors, allowing them to decide not only whether to charge suspects and what charges to bring, but also permitting them to conclude plea and sentence agreements if the accused discloses his crimes and agrees to testify as a state's witness.

the post-TRC mandate. Near the end of 2004, however, the NPA suspended its prosecutorial efforts in apartheid-era cases while it formulated a set of amended guidelines for such prosecutions.[95] Approved in December 2005, the amended prosecutions policy affirmed and expanded the NDPP's discretion to utilize a standard arrangement already at its disposal: truth in exchange for plea and sentence arrangements. Some observers contend that the policy also allowed political considerations to play a central role in determining when plea agreements are appropriate, which was not permitted under the pre-existing prosecutorial power. The policy was met with strong criticism from civil society, on the grounds that the amended guidelines so closely mirrored the amnesty provisions of the TRC Act as to amount to a repeat of the truth-for-amnesty process, and led to a constitutional challenge.[96]

III. The Amended Prosecutions Policy

The amended guidelines built upon an existing policy that already allowed for a significant amount of prosecutorial discretion. Section Four of the original policy emphasized that any decision about proceeding with a prosecution demands care because each prosecution carries profound consequences for victims, witnesses, the accused, and their families, and because prosecutorial decisions affect confidence in the judicial system.[97] The original policy also noted that while resources must be expended to vigorously pursue cases worthy of prosecution, they should not be wasted on inappropriate cases; only cases with sufficient admissible evidence to provide a reasonable prospect of conviction should be filed.[98] The original policy further recognized that the public interest may sometimes best be served by not pursuing a case, even if sufficient evidence exists, and that not all provable cases can or should be prosecuted.

In determining whether or not a prosecution is in the public interest,

---

[95] This moratorium on investigations and prosecutions while the new policy was created amounted to a permanent denial of justice in many cases. Pursuant to Section 18 of the Criminal Procedure Act (Act No. 51 of 1977), the time period in which certain cases could be prosecuted ended during the moratorium, making those cases permanently ineligible for prosecution.

[96] "South Africa: 10 Years After the Truth Commission Survivors are Frustrated," Integrated Regional Information Networks, http://www.irinnews.org/InDepthMain.aspx?InDepthId=7&ReportId=59489&Country=Yes.

[97] Prosecutions Policy, Section 4, Criteria Governing the Decision to Prosecute.

[98] *Ibid.*

the original policy instructs prosecutors to consider three main factors: (1) the nature and seriousness of the offense, including its effect on the victim, the motivation of the perpetrator, its impact on public security, and the likely outcome of a conviction; (2) the interests of the victim and the broader community, including the attitude of the victim towards prosecution, the reality that some crimes should be prosecuted regardless of a complainant's wish not to proceed, the need for deterrence, and the necessity of maintaining confidence in the judicial system; and (3) the circumstances of the offender, including criminal background, whether the accused has shown repentance or agreed to cooperate in the investigation or prosecution of others, and whether there has been an unreasonably long delay in instituting the prosecution.[99]

A. The Foundation for the Amended Policy

The amended policy, which is an appendix to the original policy described above, begins by outlining the context and background relevant to its promulgation. The NPA recognizes, in the introduction to the amended policy, that a continuation of the TRC's amnesty process would violate the Constitution in that it would "amount to a suspension of the victims' rights and would fly in the face of the objectives of the TRC process."[100] The introduction also states that those who wish to expose the truth about the conflicts of the past are free to work with the NPA "as part of the normal legal process"[101] and may "enter into agreements that are standard in the normal execution of justice and the prosecuting mandate."[102] The introduction then explains that the amended policy gives consideration to:

- The human rights culture, which underscores the Constitution and the status accorded to victims by the TRC and other legislation;
- The process of transformation to democracy, which recognized the need to create a mechanism where perpetrators could apply for amnesty (the TRC process);
- The judgment of the Constitutional Court in the *Azapo* case,[103] which

---

[99] *Ibid.*

[100] Prosecuting Policy and Directives Relating to Prosecution of Offences Emanating from Conflicts of the Past and Which Were Committed on or Before 11 May 1994, promulgated Dec. 1, 2005, Appendix A, Section A(1)(b) (hereinafter "Prosecutions Policy").

[101] *Ibid.*, Appendix A, Section A(3).

[102] *Ibid.*, Appendix A, Section A(1)(c).

[103] *Azanian Peoples Organization (AZAPO) and Others v. President of the Republic of South*

53

confirmed the constitutionality of the TRC process partly on the grounds that it did not deprive victims of the right to prosecution where the alleged perpetrators failed to apply for or were refused amnesty;
- The recommendation by the TRC that the NPA should prosecute those who failed to apply for amnesty or who were refused amnesty;
- The judgment of the Constitutional Court in the *Basson* case,[104] which held that the NPA represents the community and is under an international legal obligation to prosecute crimes of apartheid;
- The constitutional obligations of the NPA to exercise its functions without fear, favour, or prejudice;
- The right of persons affected by the decisions of the NPA to make representations to the NPA; and
- The criteria for the granting of amnesty as applied by TRC's Amnesty Committee.[105]

The introduction also asserts that the "government did not intend to mandate the NDPP, under the auspice of his or her own office, to perpetuate the TRC amnesty process."[106] This section also makes reference to "existing legislation and normal process"[107] upon which the policy relies, including:

- Section 204 of the Criminal Procedure Act (Act No. 51 of 1977), pursuant to which a person guilty of criminal conduct may testify on behalf of the state against his or her co-conspirators. If the Court trying the matter finds that he or she testified satisfactorily, it may grant indemnity from prosecution;[108]
- Section 105A of the Criminal Procedure Act (Act No. 51 of 1977), which provides that a person who has committed a criminal offence may enter into a mutually acceptable guilty plea and sentence agreement with the NPA. For apartheid-era crimes, a plea and sentence agreement requires complete disclosure in the form of a written, sworn affidavit or "solemn affirmation" from the perpetrator

---

Africa and Others, 1996 (4) SA 671 (Const. Ct.).
[104] *State v. Basson,* 2005 (1) SA 171 (Const. Ct.).
[105] Prosecutions Policy, Appendix A, Section A(2).
[106] *Ibid.,* Appendix A, Section A(3).
[107] *Ibid.*
[108] *Ibid.,* Appendix A, Section A(3)(a).

to the NDPP;[109] and

- Section 179(5) of the Constitution, pursuant to which the NDPP
  (1) must set prosecution policy in consultation with the Minister of
  Justice and the Directors of Public Prosecutions, (2) must issue policy
  directives to be observed in the prosecution process, and (3) may
  review a decision to prosecute or not to prosecute.[110]

The introduction then outlines when the NPA may exercise its
discretion not to prosecute, even if a *prima facie* case has been established.
The factors to be considered are very similar to those already provided for
in the existing policy, and include whether the victim desires prosecution,
the severity of the crime in question, the strength of the case, the cost of
the prosecution weighed against the sentence likely to be imposed, and the
interests of the community.[111] The introduction concludes with a reference to
the equality protections contained in the Constitution and the intention that
the conflicts of the past be addressed on a "rational, uniform, effective and
reconciliatory basis."[112]

B. Procedural Requirements of Plea Bargains

The amended policy outlines a list of procedural steps that "must be
strictly adhered to in respect of persons wanting to make representations to the
NDPP."[113] This process is much more detailed than anything contained in the
original policy. An individual facing prosecution for apartheid-era crimes who
wishes to "enter into arrangements with the NPA" must submit an application
in the form of a written affidavit or "solemn affirmation."[114] All representations
must contain "a full disclosure of all the facts" in relation to the offence for
which a plea arrangement is sought, including all information which may
"uncover any network, person or thing" which poses a threat to security.[115]

The NDPP must approve all decisions concerning which apartheid-
era cases will be investigated and prosecuted,[116] and must also be consulted

---

109 *Ibid.*, Appendix A, Section A(3)(b).
110 *Ibid.*, Appendix A, Section A(3)(c).
111 *Ibid.*, Appendix A, Section A(4).
112 *Ibid.*, Appendix A, Section A(5).
113 *Ibid.*, Appendix A, Section B(1).
114 *Ibid.*, Appendix A, Section B(1).
115 *Ibid.*, Appendix A, Section B(3).
116 *Ibid.*, Appendix A, Section B(7).

regarding all plea bargain arrangements and any offers made to perpetrators to become State witnesses.[117] Before reaching a decision about whether or not to prosecute, the NDPP must consult with victims as far as reasonably possible, and may consult with any private or public person or institution, including the security services.[118]

A decision not to prosecute and the reasons for that choice must be made public.[119] More broadly, the NDPP may make public statements about any matter where such statements "are necessary in the interests of good governance and transparency," but only after informing the Minister of Justice.[120] An accused person may make further representations to the NDPP requesting the withdrawal of charges once a prosecution has been instituted. The victims must, as far as reasonably possible, be consulted in any such further process.[121] The policy also requests that other State agencies refrain from using information obtained from an alleged offender through this process in any subsequent criminal trial against that individual.[122]

In order to execute the procedures outlined in the amended policy, a Task Team was created in October 2006 to assist the NPA in investigating and prosecuting apartheid-era cases. That team consisted of two advocates from within the PCLU, as well as three representatives from the National Intelligence Agency, two representatives from the SAP, one representative from the Justice Department, and one representative from the Scorpions. Cases under consideration for prosecution by the NPA are presented to the Task Team for input and feedback based on the various departments' expertise, and the team then debates whether to proceed with a prosecution. However, the ultimate decision about whether to pursue any prosecution remains solely with the NDPP.[123]

C. Criteria Governing Decisions to Prosecute

In cases stemming from apartheid-era crimes, specific criteria governing the decision to prosecute (or not to prosecute) are to be applied

---

[117] *Ibid.*, Appendix A, Section B(8).
[118] *Ibid.*, Appendix A, Section B(9).
[119] *Ibid.*, Appendix A, Section B(10).
[120] *Ibid.*, Appendix A, Section B(12).
[121] *Ibid.*, Appendix A, Section B(13).
[122] *Ibid.*, Appendix A, Section B(15).
[123] International Human Rights Clinic interview with two NPA Prosecutors (names withheld), Pretoria, South Africa, Mar. 26, 2008.

"in a balanced way."[124] First, the alleged offence must have been committed on or prior to May 11, 1994.[125] Second, the NPA must ascertain whether a prosecution can be initiated on the strength of adequate evidence, measured by the general factors contained in the existing prosecutions policy.[126] If these two threshold criteria are met, the NPA then considers the following additional criteria specific to apartheid-era crimes:

- Whether there was full disclosure by the offender;
- The relationship of the offence to a political objective;
- The extent of the offender's cooperation;
- The personal circumstances of the offender, including his or her credibility, degree of remorse, degree of indoctrination, and humanitarian considerations (such as ill health);
- The seriousness of the offence;
- The extent to which prosecution or non-prosecution will facilitate or undermine nation-building through transformation, reconciliation, development, and reconstruction;
- The extent to which prosecution may further traumatize victims; and
- The nature of the offender's role in the TRC process.[127]

A final provision empowers the NPA to consider "any further criteria, which might be deemed necessary . . . in reaching a decision",[128] indicating the significant discretion granted to prosecutors under the amended policy.

Many of the criteria guiding the NPA in its prosecutorial decisions in apartheid-era cases closely mirror those in the TRC Act's section on amnesty mechanisms and procedures. Specifically, the Amnesty Committee of the TRC also examined whether the applicant made a full disclosure, whether the act in question was associated with a political objective, the gravity of the act, and the context of the act.[129] As will be discussed below, these overlaps between the NPA policy and the TRC Act sparked vocal criticism and resulted in a constitutional challenge.

---

[124] Prosecutions Policy, Appendix A, Section C(3).

[125] *Ibid.*, Appendix A, Section C(1).

[126] *Ibid.*, Appendix A, Section C(2).

[127] *Ibid.*, Appendix A, Sections C(a)-(h).

[128] *Ibid.*, Appendix A, Section C(3)(j).

[129] Promotion of National Unity and Reconciliation Act, Chapter 4, Section 20.

D. Explanation of the Policy by the NDPP and NPA

What's different from the TRC is that amnesty made the perpetrator immune from all prosecution. But under the new amendments to the guidelines, if the victim wants to carry out a private prosecution, to pay [out of his own pocket] to have a criminal proceeding, that option is still available. Also, indemnity does not close off civil suits. If a victim still wants to proceed, there are private prosecutions.

Anonymous
NPA Prosecutor
Pretoria, October 2006

When the amended policy came into force, then-NDPP Vusi Pikoli emphasized that it gave effect to the principles outlined by President Mbeki in his 2003 speech. Specifically, Pikoli maintained that the amended policy provided no general amnesty. Although many perpetrators did not participate in the TRC, Pikoli noted that there was to be no other amnesty process so as to protect the constitutional rights of victims of gross human rights violations. Rather, he maintained, the NPA intended to pursue any case that it believed deserved prosecution and could be prosecuted, but would leave open the opportunity for perpetrators to come forward, divulge the truth, and thereby enter into plea agreements. Further, Pikoli stressed that when legal arrangements between the NPA and particular perpetrators were considered, the involvement of the victims would be crucial in determining the appropriate course of action.[130]

Pikoli also noted that the amended policy was the product of consultations with other law enforcement agencies, the Minister of Justice and Constitutional Development, the Directors of Public Prosecutions, and Unit Heads within the NPA, and was submitted to the Minister, the Cabinet, and Parliament for review and approval.[131] He emphasized that the policy drew on processes already established in the existing NPA policy "and the fact that such processes would not indemnify a person from private prosecution or civil

---

[130] Statement by Advocate Vusi Pikoli, National Director of Public Prosecutions, "On the Amended Prosecution Policy and Directives Relating to Prosecution of Criminal Matters Arising From Conflicts of the Past," Jan. 24, 2006, http://www.info.gov/za/speeches/2006/06021012261002.htm.

[131] *Ibid.*

liability. Therefore, if someone feels aggrieved regarding the process followed by the NPA, it can be tested in court."[132] However, alternative processes to government-initiated prosecutions seem to offer little hope of achieving justice. Civil claims have prescribed, and no individual victim or civil society group has yet marshaled the resources to launch private prosecutions, which are theoretically available within the legal system.

NPA prosecutors presented the amended guidelines as an opportunity to secure plea and sentence agreements that could reveal previously unknown truths about apartheid-era crimes.[133] The policy has also been portrayed as merely one component of a larger legal and political framework for preventing crime while confronting the legacy of apartheid.[134] Thus, the NPA explicitly has tied the amended policy to the country's "human rights culture," constitutional protections, and jurisprudence.[135]

IV. THE CONSTITUTIONAL CHALLENGE TO THE AMENDED PROSECUTIONS POLICY

I think that there has to be space for some form of prosecution . . . for people to say I think I've done wrong. We have to figure out how, and I don't know how long it will take us. If we are pursuing prosecutions, we need to be very clear about which crimes we want to respond to with prosecutions. We must understand that the amended policy is politically driven—not that South

---

[132] *Ibid.*

[133] International Human Rights Clinic interview with two NPA Prosecutors (names withheld), Pretoria, South Africa, Mar. 26, 2008.

[134] In this regard, the amended policy should be considered in tandem with Strategy 2020, the NPA's new approach to confront the twin problems of poverty and crime. The strategy is outcome-driven and thus seeks to devise mechanisms to resolve lingering cases. The strategy further recognizes that because the NPA faces an extremely heavy caseload, limited resources will preclude pursuit of all prosecutorial avenues. If apartheid-era crimes are seen as one of many equally pressing and competing priorities, the amended prosecutions policy might be understood as part of a broader effort to efficiently allocate scarce resources by closing older, persistent cases. For more information on Strategy 2020, see http://www.npa.gov.za/ReadContent455.aspx.

[135] Prosecutions Policy, Appendix A, Section A(2).

Africa is unique in that area. It is a bit difficult to look at those amendments in a vacuum.

Anonymous
Instructor of Law
Durban, January 2007

The amended prosecutions policy drew immediate skepticism from lawyers, victims, and civil society, leading to a constitutional challenge launched in July 2007. The lead applicant in the constitutional challenge is Thembisile Nkadimeng, the surviving sister of Nokuthula Simelane, a former MK cadre who disappeared in 1983 after being brutally tortured by apartheid-era security forces. Her father, Mathew Simelane, told the TRC's Human Rights Violations Committee in 1997 that "…what we want now are her remains so we could bury Nokuthula in a decent way. In our culture we bury people decently and we would like to do that."[136] More than a decade later, her family's wish has not yet been realized, and they have grown weary of confronting barriers that obscure the full truth about her disappearance.

Many South Africans feel a similar lack of resolution about the atrocities to which they and their loved ones were subjected during apartheid. The legal challenge to the prosecution guidelines is motivated in part by this absence of closure, and in part by a desire to participate in and influence policy decisions about the prosecution of apartheid-era crimes. The applicants thus initiated their claim pursuant to Section 38(c) of the Constitution,[137] "on behalf of all victims and all families of victims of criminal acts perpetrated by members and agents of the Apartheid regime and its security forces."[138]

The applicants first have argued that the amended prosecutions policy is a "re-run" of the TRC process that creates a second opportunity for perpetrators to gain amnesty, in violation of the TRC's promise that amnesty would be conditional and limited in time and scope. They have maintained that because the policy allows the NPA not to prosecute, regardless of the

---

[136] Testimony of Mathew Simelane before the Truth and Reconciliation Commission, June 7, 1997, http://www.doj.gov.za/trc/hrvtrans/leandra/simelane.htm.

[137] This section entitles any person or group claiming that the Bill of Rights has been violated to bring legal action.

[138] *Thembisile Nkadimeng and Others v. National Director of Public Prosecutions and Others*, High Court of South Africa (Transvaal Provincial Division), Case No. 32709/07, Founding Affidavit, para. 26 (hereinafter "Founding Affidavit").

evidence and wishes of the victims, it amounts to effective indemnity for persecutors. Second, they have argued that the amended policy violates basic rule of law principles. Specifically, by failing to prosecute and punish perpetrators, the State may damage the rule of law by creating a perception that victims cannot obtain justice, that politically-motivated or apartheid-era crimes are not serious or worthy of prosecution, that crime is a legitimate political tool, or that perpetrators can act with impunity.[139] Third, the applicants have contended that the amended policy violates a number of substantive rights protected in the Constitution's Bill of Rights, including the rights to dignity, life, freedom, security of the person, and equal protection before the law. Fourth, the applicants have asserted that the promulgation of the amended policy was procedurally improper under the constitutional separation of powers because the executive was extensively involved in drafting the policy,[140] as well as improper under the constitutional right to administrative justice[141] and the Promotion of Administrative Justice Act ("PAJA").[142] The applicants have further challenged both the impetus for the policy and the fact that victims were not included in the process. Finally, the applicants have argued that the effective indemnity created by the amended policy violates South Africa's obligations under international law.

A. The Amended Prosecutions Policy as a "Re-Run" of the TRC Amnesty Process

A core question at the center of the constitutional challenge has been whether the amended policy effectively creates a "re-run" of the TRC amnesty process. The applicants have not quibbled with the NPA's authority under the Criminal Procedure Act to reach plea agreements under section 105A or to offer indemnity under section 204, because both sections apply only after a prosecution is initiated. Instead, the applicants have focused on situations in which a decision is made not to prosecute at all.[143] Thus, the applicants' case has not been about the validity of prosecutorial discretion, but rather about

---

[139] *Thembisile Nkadimeng and Others v. National Director of Public Prosecutions and Others*, High Court of South Africa (Transvaal Provincial Division), Case No. 32709/07, Applicants' Heads of Argument, para. 8.2 (hereinafter "Applicants' Heads of Argument").
[140] South Africa Const., art. 41.
[141] *Ibid.*, art. 33.
[142] Promotion of Administrative Justice Act (Act No. 3 of 2000).
[143] Applicants' Heads of Argument, para. 2.2.

which criteria should be considered when exercising such discretion.[144]

Under Section 21(1) of the NPA Act, the NDPP is directed to "determine prosecution policy" and to "issue policy directives."[145] The applicants have argued that the NPA Act, although granting some discretion, does not allow the NDPP to decline to prosecute when sufficient evidence exists.[146] The applicants therefore have maintained that the amended policy dramatically expands the scope of the NPA's discretion and the universe of cases in which the NPA can decide not to prosecute.[147] This is especially problematic because the final decision in these instances is not reviewable by a court, unlike typical NPA decisions about indemnity and plea bargains.[148]

Thus, the applicants have contended that "[p]roperly interpreted, the policy amendments allow the prosecution authorities to decline to prosecute the perpetrators of serious crimes, even where there is sufficient evidence to secure a conviction . . . and would constitute a *de facto* indemnification from criminal liability for the crimes in question."[149] The applicants have charged that this discretion is particularly inappropriate because it may not be checked even in critical circumstances, such as when there is sufficient evidence to charge and to convict a perpetrator, the crime is severe, the victim desires prosecution, or the perpetrator did not seek or receive amnesty from the TRC.[150] In bringing their case, they seek to limit the NPA's discretion to decline to prosecute apartheid-era cases, and to signal that the NPA must devise and implement policy with adequate consultation and representation from interested stakeholders.

B. The High Court's Decision

On December 12, 2008, Judge Francis Legodi of the High Court in Pretoria ruled for the applicants and struck down the amended prosecutions policy as unconstitutional. The court accepted that, on its face, the policy could be utilized to effectively grant amnesty. As the court asked rhetorically, "if indeed the policy amendments are not intended to authorize the first respondent [NDPP] to grant indemnity or amnesty, why then the need for

---

[144] *Ibid.*, para. 2.3
[145] National Prosecution Act (Act No. 32 of 1998), para. 21(1).
[146] Applicants' Heads of Argument, para. 10.4.
[147] *Ibid.*, para. 10.7.
[148] *Ibid.*, para. 5.
[149] *Ibid.*, para. 1.2.1.
[150] Founding Affidavit, paras. 40.1-40.4.

the amendments?"[151] The court answered its own question by noting that the amended policy would "allow the first respondent even where there is a strong case and adequate evidence not to prosecute. This is contrary to the first respondent's constitutional obligation to ensure that those who are alleged to have committed offenses are prosecuted."[152] The court determined that, "Entitlement by the [NDPP] to refuse to prosecute where there is a strong case and adequate evidence to do so would in my view be unconstitutional."[153]

Even taking as true the NDPP's assertion that he would comply with the constitutional mandate to prosecute, the court found no such intention in the amended guidelines.[154] "[T]he real issue as I see it is whether the policy amendments which do not properly reflect the intention of the respondents should be allowed to remain in the book. I do not think so."[155] The court ruled that the policy amendments did in effect amount to a "copy-cat" of the TRC amnesty conditions[156] and determined that many of the criteria contained in the amended guidelines, which closely mirror those contained in the TRC Act, "are not relevant in deciding whether or not to prosecute."[157]

Finally, the court found that the case was ripe for judicial decision: "I do not think that anyone connected with the commission of the crimes cited in the applicants' papers need to be arrested before the applicants could be entitled to bring the application on the basis that their application would then be ripe or not academic. The essence of the application as I see it is promoted by the introduction of the policy amendments."[158] The court also rejected the respondents' submission that the amended policy did not amount to an effective indemnity because it left the door open for private prosecutions. As the court stated, "Crimes are not investigated by victims. It is the responsibility of the police and prosecution authority to ensure that cases are properly investigated and prosecuted. Victims of crimes rely on these institutions for investigation and prosecution. . . . [T]he essence of the complaint is that the policy amendments allow the first respondent not to prosecute even in

---

[151] *Nkadimeng et al. v. National Director of Public Prosecutions et al.*, Judgment of the High Court of South Africa, Transvaal Provincial Division, Case No. 32709/07, Dec. 12, 2008, para. 15.3.2.
[152] *Ibid.*, para. 15.4.4.
[153] *Ibid.*
[154] *Ibid.*, para. 14.1.1.
[155] *Ibid.*, para. 15.4.4.1.
[156] *Ibid.*, para. 15.4.3.1.
[157] *Ibid.*, para. 15.5.2.
[158] *Ibid.*, para. 16.2.3.1.

circumstances where there is a prima facie case."[159]

On May 4, 2009, the High Court dismissed an application by the NDPP and Minister of Justice for leave to appeal the ruling. Although the respondents could still file a special petition to the Supreme Court of Appeal or a special application for leave to appeal directly to the Constitutional Court, the ruling again confirms the obligation to pursue apartheid-era cases, particularly those in which amnesty was denied. This decision represents a major victory for the applicants, but its practical effect on the prosecution of apartheid-era crimes remains uncertain.

V. CONCLUSION

Although the High Court's ruling narrows the scope of the discretion that prosecutors can exercise over apartheid-era cases, the NPA will continue to confront difficult questions about how to balance numerous competing factors in determining which cases to pursue. The Reflections at the conclusion of this chapter touch on some of the most prominent tensions. Former TRC Commissioner Yasmin Sooka, for example, asserts that prosecutors retain too much discretion, and insists that to uphold the rule of law at least some perpetrators of gross human rights violations must be tried and imprisoned. She does not believe that apartheid-era prosecutions fundamentally threaten South Africa's stability and emphasizes the importance of consultation and transparency as the NPA works to determine how its prosecutorial powers will be exercised. Law professor Robin Palmer discusses a lack of political will and the overtly political calculations that may influence prosecutorial decisions, which he links to the threat that evenhanded prosecutions against both ANC and NP operatives could undermine the current government. Finally, an anonymous former SADF solider reveals the deep emotional scars he still carries, which have been caused by his sense of guilt and his struggle to forgive himself. His conflict is palpable: he asserts that those who set policy and gave orders must be held accountable because their acceptance of responsibility would allow lower-level officials to begin to heal themselves, yet he insists that reconciliation has largely been achieved and that so much time has elapsed that the door to the past should remain firmly shut. These narratives demonstrate that many South Africans continue to carry strong feelings on these issues, while at the same time they can make

---

[159] *Ibid.*, para. 16.2.3.3.

thoughtful contributions about how apartheid-era prosecutions should be structured and pursued.

REFLECTION

"In South Africa, we have to be careful of a slide into impunity."

Yasmin Sooka, Former TRC Commissioner, Attorney
Pretoria, October 2006

The issue [of prosecutions] has always been a difficult one because much as there was a political commitment to prosecute, I seriously question whether there was ever an intention on the part of the political parties to give effect to that commitment. Or perhaps their position was colored by an inability to prosecute political cases.

If you consider the history of what has happened from 1996 to now, it raises questions about the legitimacy of the judges. The trial of the former Minister of Defence showed institutions of the State still being managed by apartheid actors. All this was compounded by the prosecution of Wouter Basson.[160] Does the prosecution team understand the complexity of how you prosecute [apartheid-era crimes]? They use the excuse that the judge had a relative sympathy to the old regime. But you have to prepare to get an apartheid-style judge.

Mbeki wasn't interested in following through on the work of the TRC. Mbeki thinks the TRC has done its work, and that we need to put the issues away. Civil society argues that we must honor our commitment. If you look at the South African Constitution, it is premised on the notion of participation. The first problem for us is the kind of furtiveness with which the guidelines were prepared. The second problem was the lack of consultation with the victims and civil society. The State needs to say who they consulted with [in formulating the guidelines]. The third problem is the form the guidelines take. They use guidelines rather than legislation. Even the mechanism they chose is designed to avoid scrutiny.

The NPA already has fairly wide discretion to make decisions. They have the ability to use State witness and plea bargaining options. The rhetoric is that these [amended guidelines] are not another amnesty. But clearly, the

---

[160] Known in the press as "Doctor Death," Basson is a cardiologist who served as the head of Project Coast, South Africa's secret biological and chemical weapons program during apartheid. Basson and the project were allegedly involved in attacks and assassinations of anti-apartheid activists in South Africa, Namibia, Angola, and Mozambique. He was brought to trial in 1999 on charges including murder, but after a 30-month trial the presiding judge dismissed all charges.

guidelines give amnesty on a basis wider than the judges in court can give. With the guidelines, it is a public official who makes the decision [to grant amnesty]. The provisions are wider than anything we've seen before and clearly violate international law. What is needed now is more consultation around what is necessary and what is required. [In an alternate process,] there would be a mechanism to test when the prosecutor exercises discretion, to test whether the decision was an appropriate one. There should be a mechanism to review the [prosecutor's] decision. If they really feel the discretion is necessary, why not appoint a judge to sit on an ad hoc basis to make those decisions? In South Africa, we have to be careful of a slide into impunity.

We traversed this road before with the TRC and still did not have answers. In the absence of answers, what is left? If the TRC process had to be tested then the prosecution process has to be tested. Prosecutions might threaten stability, but the wall hasn't fallen yet. Yes, there are strong interest groups who try to subvert the process, but it needs to be done. There is a great deal of unhappiness in the Afrikaner community. Bitterness, feelings of betrayal by the process, de Kock wanting to know why he's sitting there paying the price. The ones who have borne the stigma of apartheid are the ordinary foot soldiers.

I'm not sure how many amnesty-seekers [who testified before the TRC] were genuinely there because they wanted to be. You mustn't romanticize the process. They came forward kicking and screaming. I have no romances that this process necessarily leads to reconciliation. People didn't get satisfaction. There were alliances of the elites on both sides. Who betrayed whom? People sold out and were bought over. White people were tainted. There was a whole load of victims who have been left with nothing, and prosecutions can fill this gap. People want to know that there is accountability.

Reflection

"A vigorous prosecutions policy, where we had nothing for seven or eight years, would seem a bit strange."

Robin Palmer, Professor of Law
Durban, January 2007

During the TRC process, I was involved basically as a consultant in the background, on the academic, judicial, and law sides. The problem I had was that the focus of [the] TRC was mainly reconciliation. They bent over backwards to accommodate people, to get them involved, to bring them out. The follow-up was not strong enough for those who abused the system. And that was mainly because the composition of the TRC. [It] was head[ed] by Desmond Tutu and Alex Boraine, who were very strong on reconciliation. Those guys were coming from a "let's get together" perspective. Mandela was very strong on uniting society, so they didn't want to use the TRC as a stick, only as a carrot.

There was a lot of political pressure on Tutu and the Commission to wrap things up quickly and to make a nice sound-bite out of it. But it confirmed what people had been saying all along: descriptions of torture, admissions of torture, and all of those things. It had a cleansing effect to some extent. There were many security force guys who didn't apply for amnesty. There are many guys in positions of power who should have been prosecuted. There are many people who committed murders sitting as community policemen around this province.

The problem was that the follow-up was a bit of a shambles because of a lack of structured policy around what to do for the people who didn't come. They should have had a policy in place saying that for those who don't apply for amnesty, this is what is going to happen to you: vigorous prosecution. Any *prima facie* case we will prosecute to the nth degree, including P.W. Botha, who just completely ignored the process. The whole point about it is that if you don't have follow-up, there is no closure for the people, those people murdered and destroyed. [The NPA] keeps changing the policy guidelines. You will find that South Africans are brilliant at bureaucracy and setting up guidelines but very bad at implementation. So there is massive dissonance between what is written and what is happening on the ground. This can be seen in our AIDS policy, prisons policy, and the implementation of prosecutions.

The biggest problem with our prosecutions policy can be summed up in a nutshell: political appointments to the top jobs. The problem was that the national prosecutions head is a political appointee, which meant that all the career officers were below him and final decision-making on the essential cases was by a political appointee who came from the ANC's inner circle, and therefore he was compromised. So loyalty won over on prosecutions policy. The ANC had some skeletons in their cupboard from their camps, and they didn't want to be too vigorous in case they had to be prosecuted, so they preferred it to die a slow death. They didn't want an evenhanded approach. And of course the TRC commissioners were mainly ANC-aligned, and naturally so because of the transition and transformation, and Mandela's approach to try to unify the country.

For the most part, in most cases, the provincial directors [in the NPA] are left to do their own thing. When you get to sensitive cases like Jacob Zuma's, for example, it goes to the NDPP for final decision. Even the Scorpions, through their director, report directly to the NDPP. It is a bit of hybrid situation, you've got lawyers, prosecutors, and policemen in the same wing. The problem is, in my view, that the guardians of society are not independent people of character, they are political appointees. What you really need at the head of the units are vigorous, fearless, Ralph Nader[161] types, and what you actually have are loyalists who for the most part are scared of rocking the boat, so there is no real protection. Therefore, the prosecutions authority, the public protector, and prosecutions policy are all influenced by not rocking the boat when it comes to the ruling party. They could still [undertake prosecutions], but there is no political will to prosecute aggressively. That's the problem with the boat: the political will to aggressively prosecute has already sailed.

If you prosecute aggressively, some will say, "So if you are prosecuting all the apartheid-era guys, what about the ANC camps and what about all the people who committed abuses there?" I think there was incredible abuse of women and summary execution and all kinds of things in ANC camps, so they are scared of vigorously following that up as well. For instance, many cabinet ministers know of colleagues who used to be informers for the police. It is just too hurtful and divisive to force the issue.

There is a wealth of information that hasn't been used. There is an enormous amount of evidence, but [prosecutions require] a lot of resources. Also the time has passed; we have now gone ten years. To now suddenly have

---

[161] American attorney and political activist renowned for calling attention to government and corporate corruption.

a vigorous prosecutions policy, where we had nothing for seven or eight years, would seem a bit strange. Everyone would say it was politically-motivated victimization. That chapter effectively closed with the death of P.W. Botha. He was the guy in charge of the entire joint management system, which treated government as a "total onslaught" situation. They should have arrested him; no reason why not. Right up to his death, he was defiant and unrepentant about what he did. I think they also had their political constraints about what they could and could not do. I think the idea of reinvigorating a prosecutions strategy would be a double-edged sword.

REFLECTION

"[We] have to reconcile ourselves with ourselves."

Anonymous, Former SADF Soldier
Pretoria, January 2007

I grew up in Rhodesia on a farm, but in the mid-1970s my folks decided that the situation was no longer safe and, like most white people in Rhodesia, emigrated south. I was a Rhodesian citizen, and laws had just been passed in the late 1970s that [said] if you wanted to become a South African citizen, you had to serve in the military or stay in the country for five years and do national service. So we decided as a bunch of young guys that we would go to the military straight out of school. We were put into infantry units, which are elite fighting units, then joined special operations units that typically did things that the standard infantry units didn't do. We were deployed behind the lines either by parachute, helicopter, or sea. I operated in various countries— what we called then the frontline states—very much covert, undercover. To this day, the previous government maintains that 90% of that stuff didn't happen. At the end of that process, I took a permanent [military] position because I didn't know what else to do in life and I quite enjoyed what I was doing. I was appointed as an officer because I was by then a South African citizen. I spent the next four and a half years in a special operations unit targeting specifically the eastern side of Africa: Mozambique, Tanzania, and the Eastern Highlands of Zimbabwe.

In 1987, by the time I had attained the rank of a full captain, the unit that we were active in—contentious even then—was disbanded. The reasoning given was that the government did not want to have an embarrassment when the country got black majority rule. So in the late 1980s, the policymakers already knew the direction the country was going. So I basically got retrenched. That was the end of my military career. They did give us an option to continue in the military in other roles. I thought I couldn't do this; I liked being operational—I cannot sit in an office and write reports. When the government changed and they spoke about this TRC thing, I felt that we were in danger; they are going to start hunting guys through kangaroo court and jail.

After 1994 most military records were destroyed. Today if you search for details of operations or data, you won't find anything. I was an officer in a unit with 300 men under me, which comprised black, coloured, and white as well as foreign troops. All I needed was one of them to turn around in an effort to save his hide and say on that day [I] ordered the killing of one or a hundred local people, and I would spend the rest of my life—no matter whether I could prove it—saying I am innocent.

A number of guys in our regiment committed suicide in the two years after 1994, out of the pure fear of retribution. There were many things that we did that were not nice: waking a whole town of people up in the middle of the night, knocking them out of their houses, burning them down. You don't have to shoot somebody. You can do certain things that are close enough to killing somebody. With the TRC starting, I lived a number of years in absolute fear. Whenever the phone rang, I felt someone was fishing. How can we pull you into it? What role did you play? Were you ever in the military? We kept very low key, didn't apply for promotions, just did our job. The first couple of years you were asked, "What was your role?" I'm a white male, what do you think my role was? White South Africans, friends of ours, were turning around and saying, "You guys are killers." But we kept them safe at home while their fathers bought them out of military service or kept them studying. [They were] turning around and saying, "We don't want anything to do with you because you are this tainted lot."

My sense of the TRC has changed as I have done a lot of development work within the country in the last five years. Just before 1994 there was a tremendous feeling amongst ex-military men that the government was selling us out. A lot of us didn't agree with what F.W. [de Klerk] had to say; we thought that he was an ANC pushover. We were winning, so why the sudden about turn? There was a lot of resentment that sat there for a long time. I was proud of what I did, I was an officer, and as much of a gentleman that I could be. I followed instructions because if I didn't I would have been shot, put in front of the firing squad. Yes, you can make a moral choice, but sometimes it is hard to see this choice as clearly as [we do] now. We followed orders when they were clear and not bad or unjust. Today, it looks as though some of us were not strong enough to make those moral choices.

I got married in the late 1990s and one day my wife came across my military uniform. I started explaining to my wife what we did—[it] was a bit of a healing process. In discussing with my wife, and as the TRC began to unpack, something came out of the TRC that changed my view of the war period. I [had] seen many atrocities perpetrated by both sides on their own people. I had come across incidents where terrorists had perpetrated things against their own people, and we had even come across some of these in action. I learned many years later that some of the incidents may have been perpetrated by South African forces to create the impression that this is what the terrorists had done. [But] I had never witnessed or been part of this, so that may only be a rumor. A lot of this I only learned later, so there has been a tremendous developmental cycle for me.

I feel people must be held accountable for what they did. The guys at the forefront who gave the orders—General Magnus Malan, P.W. Botha— refused to go to the TRC and have been protected. They have nailed some low-level people. If they can nail a poor rifleman like Harrington,[162] what is to stop them nailing a captain that is fourteen levels above the rifleman? But the person who gave Harrington the order came off scot-free. The individuals you hold accountable should be the State President, the Minister of Police, the Minister of Justice, the cabinet of the day. Even if they had made a statement that this happened on our orders, because this was how we felt and this is what we did—whether that would absolve everyone below them or not is not important—I think that would have done a lot more for reconciliation between whites, not black and white.

There is tremendous resentment that there are people out there we know who should be hung, and they have climbed the echelons of government and business. Especially the ANC and PAC henchmen who not only perpetrated violence against us but also against their own people in training and elsewhere.

One of the things that really got me upset was Adriaan Vlok, who washed the feet of this guy [Frank Chikane]. He was Minister of Police, and the buck stopped with him for internal stuff. So if you were told to go and get activists, terrorists, insurgents, he would give the instructions. You won't find that in writing because military terminology would have been "neutralize the enemy" or the standard thing that "the problem must go away." Interpret that! They have been very clever in the way that anything written has been termed, so it is left to interpretation.

I still wouldn't have gone to the Commission even knowing what I know now because I fear for my life, and not necessarily from the ANC guys. I am not saying I know stuff that can incriminate people, but we were told in the early years that we must keep quiet and [to] the guys who had families, they'd say, "We know where your families are." So, in a way, people must be held accountable but the collateral damage that might roll out from this might be more destructive than actually locking up a single person.

---

[162] In February 1992, Constable William Harrington was sentenced to eight years in prison, which was increased to eighteen years on appeal, for torturing and assassinating ANC activist Mbongeni Jama.

Reconciliation did happen, and even if it was superficial in the beginning, it has filtered down, and you can see it to a large extent in the youth of the country today. They are not aware of race. My kids go to a school to which twenty years [ago] I would never have allowed them to go. Ninety percent of the class is black kids. And those kids don't see color, and that's great. To me that is where reconciliation has happened and will only happen, from about grade seven or eight down. Even the grade twelves, they all giggle, whether they are black, white, green, or yellow, about Britney Spears and MP3 players. "AK47" doesn't mean anything to them. The only time the lot of them are involved with an AK is when they are faced with crime. So, reconciliation in my point of view has happened. The only fight now is over who gets the Gucci jeans. And that isn't such a bad fight.

In terms of personal reconciliation . . . 90% of us have to reconcile ourselves with ourselves, and it is very hard to do that. And the baggage, it's there continuously. Some of the baggage is ludicrous: my own friends who won't accept me [because I was in the military], or my neighbor who is of Xhosa origin and won't accept me because I am a white male. All that we can do is live with it on a day-to-day basis. A lot of lives on both sides were lost. I don't have closure, and how am I going to get it?

The images are burned into my mind, images that will not go away. They are not necessaryly images of me shooting people. There's an image of a school that was raided by terrorists [or] so we were told; who did the raiding we don't know, [and] today there are reports blaming elite units of ours, but [those reports are] unproven. And the girls were raped and mutilated. We came upon this. Burn that out of my mind? You are never going to do that. My own troops dying, kids of seventeen or eighteen dying in my arms.

There is a story that death stalks you, before any dying starts, before any shooting starts, you get a funny smell and you know people are going to die. I smelled that, and sure enough some of our troops did not make it. I will be emotional until the day I die because I was involved in the killing and maiming, destruction of humans, of animals, of the countryside. When I say I can't go on, my wife says, "Just don't commit suicide." That's not an option. My kids keep me going.

Sometimes you just want to scream about those blokes who sent us out there to do that. Mothers trusted me to look after their sons, and all I could do was give them a dog tag. Although the firing has stopped, many of us live with it day-to-day, and bear the deeper psychological scars and physical scars. We are all trying to deal with it in our own ways.

I have to accept that I failed my country because the communists took over, if you want to look at that point of view, because that is who we were fighting. But twenty years down you realize that you were fighting your own countrymen, who were fighting you because they didn't know exactly what you stood for and you didn't know what they stood for. As my previous foresworn enemy, the ANC has done a lot of things that make me say you are not different from the other lot, the white government. But on the other hand, you guys actually have a big heart; [you] understand the great ramifications of the process. This is the one thing I will always forever be thankful for: the miracle of this country. Nelson Mandela turned around and said, "There is no time for this, it's happened. We can forgive, but we must never forget."

Obviously I am going to say that to save my little skin. It is easy to say it is a thing of the past, and I guess that is what I am saying to myself. Not that it must be buried and forgotten, but it needs to be put into a box of what happened. Hell, we're not happy with it, but it happened. I think the book needs to be closed now; they need to accept that it is over, that it is finished. I think there needs to be some kind of a closing statement from the TRC or somebody, saying we've gone as far as we can and in the interests of building the nation we are moving on, it is finished. But there are people on both sides who need to have some kind of reckoning, and whatever [God] they believe in they'll stand before them one day and have to answer.

CHAPTER 4

Prosecutions Policy at Work

The attitude of the victim is pivotal because if the victim will forgive, he or she may not want to proceed with the prosecutions. On the other hand, there are some crimes that are so serious that they need to be prosecuted regardless of what the victim would like.

Anonymous, NPA Prosecutor
Pretoria, October 2006

What [the lack of prosecutions] says is that government still does not want to listen to the voice of victims. Government is willing to listen to consultants, big NGOs, academics and so forth, but people from the subaltern, people from the ground, government is not willing to listen [to them]. So you find that these amnesties, this plea bargaining, might take place behind closed doors without the involvement of victims. That's our fear. In terms of the relationship between victims and government, [the amended prosecutions policy] further represents marginalization from structures of governance, democracy, and so forth. In terms of the dialogue, you will see a lot of bitterness from our members, which must be expected. People are allowed to be bitter in terms of government saying, "Let's just move on."

Tshepo Madlingozi, Legal/Advocacy Officer, Khulumani
Johannesburg, March 2008

I. INTRODUCTION

Analysis of criminal prosecutions and plea bargains both during and
after the TRC demonstrates that South Africa has not yet determined how to
consistently address the question of prosecutions for apartheid-era violations. A
lack of coherence and haphazard implementation of policy characterize the NPA's
fitful attempts to prosecute apartheid-era perpetrators, and highlight the tensions
that exist because of the interplay between the TRC and prosecutions.

The Reflections at the end of this chapter from Jan Wagener, the
attorney for Adriaan Vlok, and Dumisa Ntsebeza, an advocate and former TRC
Commissioner, illustrate the ongoing arenas of debate and contrasting attitudes
toward how much emphasis to place on looking forward versus looking back;
whether prosecutions can positively influence long term stability and the rule of
law; how much value should be placed on the rights of victims and truth-seeking;
and how evenhandedness is to be determined. Both Wagener and Ntsebeza
underline, however, the highly politicized nature of decision-making surrounding
prosecutions policy since the end of apartheid. Indeed, this may be the only area
of agreement between the two.

Several trends have appeared since 1994. Overall, there have been very
few prosecutions for apartheid-era crimes, against either high-ranking or low-
ranking officials. After its creation in 2003, the PCLU conducted an audit
of approximately 300 TRC-referred cases, of which 167 were closed on the
basis that "prosecutions could not be instituted."[163] As of 2008, the PCLU
had identified sixteen apartheid-era cases for investigation and prosecution,
although the details of such cases, and the status of their progress, are not
publicly known.[164] The fact that architects of the TRC's amnesty provision
were mistaken in expecting amnesty to encourage a flood of applications from
high-level apartheid-era officials has had no apparent effect on the number of
prosecutions. Former President P.W. Botha refused to engage seriously with the
TRC process, famously decrying it as a circus.[165] Botha's dismissive attitude was
prevalent among South Africa's apartheid-era political and military leaders, yet
very few have been pursued.

---

[163] "Profile of PCLU Cases," The National Prosecuting Authority of South Africa, http://
www.npa.gov.za/ReadContent405.aspx.
[164] Advocate Anton Ackermann, "Priority Crimes Litigation Unit (PCLU) 2007-2008 Report to Select Committee on Security and Constitutional Affairs," http://www.pmg.org.za/
files/docs/080521pclu.ppt.
[165] "HNP Aligns Itself with Defiant Botha," Daily Dispatch, Jan. 9, 1998, http://www.dis-
patch.co.za/1998/01/09/PAGE11TR.HTM.

More prosecutions—especially trials—occurred during the TRC process than after its completion in 2003. A few high-profile acquittals, most prominently that of Wouter Basson, still loom over the NPA as an institution. In addition, since the submission of the TRC's Final Report, the NPA's record on prosecutions has been marked only by two pleas bargains. One agreement involved the well-publicized and highly-charged case of Adriaan Vlok, the only former apartheid-era Cabinet member to participate in the TRC process, and the other agreement involved the virtually unknown case of the APLA Four. Together, the plea bargains and lack of trials have raised significant concerns amongst victims and human rights advocates about whether the obligation to prosecute is being fulfilled. Just as importantly, the lack of a coherent and consistent policy has left South Africans with a sense of dissatisfaction and uncertainty about the way forward.

II. INITIAL PROSECUTIONS OF APARTHEID-ERA CRIMES: PROSECUTIONS DURING THE TRC

The South African justice system began to prosecute some offenders for crimes related to apartheid during the transition to democracy, and continued to do so throughout the 1990s and 2000s, both while the TRC was active and after it ceased to operate. The number of prosecutions was never great,[166] but a few trials garnered significant public attention. Most notable were the conviction of Vlakplaas commander Eugene de Kock and the acquittals of former high-ranking defense officials Magnus Malan and Wouter Basson. Lower-profile individuals were also prosecuted, with a mixture of successes and failures.

Some commentators blamed the small number of convictions in those first years partially on the fact that many white prosecutors and judges who remained in the South African justice system after the end of apartheid were unwilling or unable to fully grasp the atrocities that had been committed.[167] A sunset clause contained in the negotiated settlement ending apartheid allowed employees of the apartheid State, including attorneys general, judges, and civil servants, to retain their positions for five years. On the other hand, substantial numbers of experienced prosecutors did resign after 1994, resulting

[166] Lovell Fernandez, "Post-TRC Prosecutions in South Africa," *Justice in Transition—Prosecution and Amnesty in Germany and South Africa* (Gerhard Werle ed., 2006), p. 65.
[167] Bill Berkeley, "The 'New' South Africa: Violence Works," *World Policy Journal*, Dec. 22, 1996, p. 73 (attributing the Malan acquittal to this cause).

in a shortage of prosecutors who were capable of dealing with the complex task of prosecuting apartheid-era offenses.[168] Some commentators also blamed the police for shielding their former colleagues from investigation.[169] The outcomes of these initial cases form the historical backdrop for current discussions about prosecutions.

A. Prosecutions of High-Profile Defendants

Probably the most successful prosecution for apartheid-era crimes was that of Eugene de Kock, commander of the notorious secret police unit known as Vlakplaas, which was involved in numerous killings, bombings, and other abuses. De Kock was convicted of six murders and numerous other crimes in 1996,[170] and remains in prison. Following his conviction, de Kock began to name police generals and government ministers, including former presidents P.W. Botha and F.W. de Klerk, as responsible for the brutal activities of the secret police.[171] He testified on this subject for twelve days, seeking mitigation of his sentence.[172] Since his conviction, de Kock has also testified at trials arising from several other apartheid-related offenses.[173] He has emphatically claimed that senior government figures from the apartheid era who did not testify at the TRC and have not been prosecuted knew about and authorized Vlakplaas's operations. For instance, de Kock testified when P.W. Botha was put on trial for ignoring a TRC subpoena, calling Botha a "coward" for his refusal to take responsibility.[174]

During the transitional period, the government also successfully prosecuted the murderers of Chris Hani, the very popular secretary general of the South African Communist Party, who had previously been an ANC military leader.[175] Hani was shot and killed in 1993 by Janusz Walus, a Polish immigrant, at the instigation of Clive Derby-Lewis, a right-wing politician in

---

[168] Fernandez, pp. 77–78.

[169] Ibid., pp. 74–75.

[170] Martin Meredith, *Coming to Terms: South Africa's Search for Truth* (New York: Public Affairs, 1999), p. 52.

[171] Ibid., pp. 52–54.

[172] Ibid.

[173] "Former Police Commissioner Rejects de Kock Allegations," S.A. Press Ass'n, July 22, 2004.

[174] Meredith, p. 187.

[175] Jan Hennop, "Chris Hani: An Assassination That Nearly Sparked Civil War in S. Africa," Agence France-Presse, April 9, 2003.

the Conservative Party.[176] In the days after the murder, at least 70 people were killed in mob violence and thousands of protesters marched.[177] There were fears that the violence would escalate into an all-out race war; Archbishop Tutu remembered it as "one of the most scary moments in our country's history."[178] Walus was arrested on the day of the killing,[179] and both men were convicted in 1993.[180] Their death sentences were commuted to life in prison when South Africa subsequently abolished the death penalty.[181] They appeared before the TRC, but the Commission denied amnesty on the grounds that they had not given a full disclosure.[182] Chris Hani's family and the Communist Party argued that there was a broader conspiracy behind the murder, which Derby-Lewis and Walus kept hidden.[183]

A high-profile prosecutorial failure—described by one newspaper as "the most politically charged courtroom drama of the decade"[184]—was the 1996 acquittal of Magnus Malan, a former defense minister. Malan was prosecuted, along with other senior military officers and IFP members, in connection with the violence between the IFP and the ANC in the late 1980s and early 1990s. Malan and other members of the military were charged with arming and training Inkatha supporters and encouraging them to attack ANC supporters.[185] The prosecutor and the judge at Malan's trial were whites who had held office under apartheid, and Malan went to trial so confident of acquittal that he advised former members of the security forces not to apply for amnesty from the TRC.[186] The judge acquitted all the defendants after a trial that many observers felt was based on insufficiently reliable prosecution evidence.[187]

Public reaction to the verdict generally split along racial lines.[188] One survivor of a massacre in which Malan was charged said, "South African law

---

[176] David Beresford, "Pardon Deadline Tempts Apartheid Guilty to Surface," *The Guardian*, Dec. 13, 1996.

[177] Hennop.

[178] *Ibid.*

[179] Nelandri Narianan, "4 Bullets for a Dream," *Pretoria News*, April 10, 2008.

[180] "Derby-Lewis' Parole Hearing Set for December," S.A. Press Ass'n, Nov. 25, 2008.

[181] *Ibid.*

[182] "Court Rejects Amnesty Appeal by Chris Hani's Killers," BBC News, May 13, 2001.

[183] "SACP Opposes Parole Hearing for Hani's Killers," S.A. Press Ass'n, Oct. 9, 2002.

[184] "Dirty War's Skeletons Still Rattle," *Financial Times*, Oct. 14, 1996.

[185] Berkeley, p. 73.

[186] *Ibid.*

[187] "Dirty War's Skeletons Still Rattle," *Financial Times*, Oct. 14, 1996.

[188] *Ibid.*

has been like this and it's always going to be like this: murderers go free."[189]
Archbishop Tutu and Alex Boraine issued a statement asserting that the trial
had demonstrated that the TRC was a more effective means than criminal
trials for uncovering the truth about the past.[190] However, after his acquittal,
Malan publicly encouraged other former members of the military not to
cooperate with the TRC.[191] The acquittal took place just six weeks before the
cutoff date for amnesty applications to the TRC.[192] Likely influenced by both
the acquittal and Malan's public statements, few members of the SADF applied
for amnesty.[193] Malan appeared before the TRC in 1997, but did not seek
amnesty and refused to answer many of the questions put to him.[194]

    Dr. Wouter Basson was another senior apartheid government figure
whose high-profile prosecution ended in acquittal. Basson was in charge of
the military's chemical and biological warfare programs, known as Project
Coast. He was charged with 229 murders, as well as other crimes ranging
from fraud to drug trafficking.[195] His acquittal on all counts in 2002, after a
30-month trial, was met by widespread disillusionment.[196] One NGO, Jubilee
South Africa, called the verdict "a shameful day for truth and justice" and
charged that "apartheid's powerful military and secret service bosses still have
much to hide and still have the means to obstruct the wheels of justice."[197] The
prosecution appealed Basson's acquittal to the Constitutional Court, which
denied the claim that the judge had been biased but reinstated certain charges
that had earlier been dismissed on jurisdictional grounds.[198] The successful
appeal opened the door for reinstated charges to be re-filed against Basson.
However, the Constitutional Court declined to decide whether, if charges were
brought again, Basson would be able to rely on the defenses of double jeopardy
and the right to a speedy trial.[199] In 2005, the NPA announced it would not re-

---

[189] David Beresford, "South Africa Reels as Malan Walks Free," *The Guardian*, Oct. 12, 1996.
[190] *Ibid.*
[191] Jeremy Sarkin, *Carrots and Sticks: The TRC and the South African Amnesty Process* (New York: Intersentia, 2004), p. 374.
[192] *Ibid.*, pp. 373–74.
[193] *Ibid.*
[194] Suzanne Daley, "Apartheid-Era Defense Chief Defends Role in Ordering Raids on Neighboring Countries," *New York Times*, May 8, 1997.
[195] Vusi Nzapheza, "Wouter Basson, Apartheid-Era Chemical and Biological Weapons Expert," *Cape Times*, Feb. 26, 2007.
[196] Sarkin, p. 376.
[197] *Ibid.*
[198] *State v. Basson* 2005 (1) SA 171 (Const. Ct.).
[199] *Ibid.*

charge Basson.[200]

B. Lower-Profile Defendants

In addition to these relatively high-profile figures, some less senior individuals were also prosecuted for apartheid-related crimes. Among these was Brian Mitchell, a police captain, convicted in 1992 for leading several constables in a massacre in 1988 at the village of Trust Feed in KwaZulu-Natal.[201] The police intended to kill a group of UDF activists in an effort to strengthen the position of the local Inkatha leadership, but they mistakenly chose the wrong house and instead killed eleven villagers who were attending a wake.[202] Mitchell was granted amnesty by the TRC in 1996 and freed from prison, whereupon he publicly sought the forgiveness of the Trust Feed community.[203] This gesture met with mixed results; some residents were outraged and rejected Mitchell's attempts,[204] but others extended forgiveness.[205] He has continued to play a public role on occasion; Archbishop Tutu has held him up as an example of someone making a genuine effort towards reconciliation.[206]

Ferdi Barnard, a member of the SADF's Civil Co-operation Bureau, was convicted in 1998 for the murder of anti-apartheid activist David Webster and received two life sentences.[207] Former security policemen Gideon Nieuwoudt, Wynand du Toit, and Marthinus Ras were convicted in 1996 for the car-bomb killing of the Motherwell Four, three black police officers and a police informer who were murdered in 1989 for allegedly leaking information to the ANC. Their amnesty application for these killings had been denied for failure to make a full disclosure, and they were sentenced to between ten and twenty years of imprisonment each.[208]

In 2002, two former Ciskei Defense Force soldiers—Lt.-Col. Vakele

---

[200] Ernest Mabuza, "Basson 'Cannot Be Tried Again on Same Charges,'" *Business Day (South Africa)*, Oct. 30, 2005.

[201] Meredith, pp. 104–07.

[202] *Ibid.*

[203] "Apartheid Killer Seeks Reconciliation," *Associated Press*, April 28, 1997.

[204] Meredith, p. 112.

[205] "Apartheid Killer Seeks Reconciliation," *Associated Press*, April 28, 1997.

[206] "Peace Can Do More Than War—Tutu," S.A. Press Ass'n, Mar. 21, 2003.

[207] "Former CCB Agent Ferdi Barnard Convicted of Murder," S.A. Press Ass'n, June 1, 1998.

[208] David Philips, "The Student, the Mother and the Security Policeman: Truth and Reconiliation in the Siphiwo Mtimkhulu case?", http://www.londongrip.com/LondonGrip/SouthAfrica_TRC(3)_by_David_Philips.html.

Archibald Mkosana and rifleman Mzamile Thomas Gonya—were acquitted of all charges in connection with the Bhisho massacre in 1992, in which troops fired on a crowd of ANC demonstrators, killing 29 and injuring over 300.[209] The TRC had previously refused amnesty to both men because they could not reasonably claim to have a political motivation when they argued that they had acted in self-defense against a crowd that posed a danger to the troops.[210] The court held, however, that under the circumstances the approaching crowd posed a danger to the troops and that the troops were entitled to fire in self-defense.[211]

Prosecutions initiated subsequent to the TRC process have faced significant procedural obstacles and apparent institutional lethargy. In 2004, three former policemen—Gideon Nieuwoudt, Johannes Martin van Zyl, and Johannes Koole—were charged with the 1984 murders of three anti-apartheid activists known as the Pebco Three.[212] The prosecution was delayed as the defendants appealed for a review of the TRC's denial of amnesty.[213] In 2007, the burnt remains of the Pebco Three were located, and physical evidence contradicted some of what the accused murderers had previously told the TRC about the manner in which the three victims were killed.[214] None of the perpetrators of the Pebco Three murders has publicly set the record straight on these discrepancies. Nieuwoudt died of cancer in 2005,[215] and the prosecution of van Zyl and Koole has not subsequently been pursued.

Two black former policemen, Pumelele Gumengu and Aaron Mtobeli Tyani, were convicted in 2005 of murdering ANC guerilla Sthembele Zokwe in 1988. Both men had been arrested soon after the killing, but they escaped the same day from different prisons and were then hired and given new identities by the SADF.[216] The TRC refused them amnesty for failure to make a full disclosure.[217]

It appears that during the 1990s and 2000s, few ANC members or

---

[209] Sarkin, p. 377.

[210] Louise Flanagan, "Vlok's Upcoming Trial Follows Several Others," *The Star*, Aug. 2, 2007.

[211] "Ciskei Troops Acquitted for Bisho Massacre," S.A. Press Ass'n, Mar. 13, 2002.

[212] Cecilia Russell, "Looking for Closure as Excavation Reveals the Bitter Past," *The Star*, Aug. 10, 2007.

[213] "Ex-Security Cop Gideon Nieuwoudt in Court," S.A. Press Ass'n, April 19, 2005.

[214] Shaun Smillie, "Come Clean on Pebco Three Now, Ex-Cops Urged," *The Star*, July 17, 2007.

[215] "Another Week," *Financial Mail*, Aug. 26, 2005.

[216] Flanagan.

[217] "Killer Policemen May Appeal," S.A. Press Ass'n, Nov. 28, 2005.

supporters—and certainly no prominent ones—were prosecuted for apartheid-related offenses. One possible exception was Buyile Ronnie Blani, a former anti-apartheid activist who was jailed for one year in 2005 under a plea bargain for the robbery and murder of two white farmers.[218] However, Blani did not apply for amnesty for this crime, making it unclear whether the crime should be considered politically motivated or not.[219]

III. Post-TRC Actions: Plea Bargains

Victims have waited far too long for justice. What is most disconcerting is while the government has stated that it will not institute another "TRC-like" process that will cater for thousands of victims who were left out of the TRC process, this [amended prosecutions] policy will have the effect of giving perpetrators a second chance.

Tshepo Madlingozi
Legal/Advocacy Officer, Khulumani
Johannesburg, July 2007

Since the TRC completed its work in 2003 and sent a list of possible perpetrators along with evidence it had gathered to the NPA, there have been no prominent trials for apartheid-era crimes. Indeed, two plea bargains—one highly publicized and one not—occupy the entire public landscape of action (or inaction) surrounding prosecutions since the amended prosecution policy came into effect in late 2005. While much attention has been paid to the amended guidelines, both plea agreements on their face rely instead on prosecutorial discretion granted under section 105A of the Criminal Procedure Act, a provision that pre-dates the guidelines. Nonetheless, the amended guidelines clearly played a defining role in both plea agreements, and together the cases illustrate the ethical tensions, practical challenges, and political constraints attendant to prosecutions of apartheid-era crimes in South Africa.

---

[218] Flanagan; "'Prosecution Frenzy' Against Apartheid Activists," Liquid Africa, May 2, 2005; "NPA Denies Blani's Sentencing Could Lead to Further Arrests," S.A. Press Ass'n, May 1, 2005.
[219] Flanagan.

A. The Case of the APLA Four

In May 2006, a little known case of four former members of APLA, the PAC's military wing, marked the first plea bargain concluded after the amended guidelines.[220] The APLA Four quietly pleaded guilty to a range of offences including murder and attempted murder committed in the course of a raid on an Eastern Cape police station. On March 28, 1994, Khwezi Ngoma, Litha Ntlabathi, Vumile Nkithi, and Mandla Phalaphala raided a Willowvale police station to obtain weapons for use in APLA operations. Police Sergeants Sobantu Tsipa and Lulama Binase confronted and resisted the invaders, and were shot. Sergeant Tsipa died; Sergeant Binase, who was injured, was the complainant in the 2006 case.

The four accused entered into a plea agreement with respect to their actions that night.[221] In mitigation, the agreement notes their relative youth at the time of the attack, their place in a command structure in which absolute deference was given to the organization's leadership-in-exile, their pursuit of the liberation of South Africa from apartheid, and their present contributions to the country as teachers, councilors, parents, and self-employed businessmen.[222] In addition, the agreement specifically states that "[t]he prosecutor has also consulted with all the relevant victims in the matter and they support this plea and sentence agreement."[223] Each accused was sentenced to a total of 28 years imprisonment on eight separate counts; all the sentences were suspended for five years.[224]

Despite being the first plea for apartheid-era crimes negotiated after the NPA's amended guidelines came into effect, the case is virtually unknown in South Africa. In contrast to the local and international media attention given to the Adriaan Vlok plea bargain, discussed below, the APLA case

---

[220] International Human Rights Clinic Interview with NPA Prosecutor (name withheld), Pretoria, South Africa, Mar. 26, 2008. According to the plain language of the plea agreement, it was concluded under Section 105A of the Criminal Procedure Act. *See* Appendix D.

[221] *See* Appendix D for the full text of the plea agreement.

[222] *In the Matter between the State and Khwezi Ngoma et al.*, High Court of South Africa (Transkei Division), Case No.125/04, Plea and Sentence Agreement, May 2, 2006, para. 12.1 *et seq.*

[223] *Ibid.*, para. 7.3.

[224] *Ibid.*, para. 15. A suspended sentence means that the perpetrator is placed on probation for the period of years of the suspension, and will not serve time in prison so long as he does not encounter additional legal troubles during the period of suspension. However, a suspended sentence still results in a criminal record, even if no time is served.

appears to have garnered only a single news story in the Eastern Cape's *Daily Dispatch*.[225]

B. The Case of Adriaan Vlok

In August 2007, Adriaan Vlok, the Minister of Law and Order from 1986 to 1991, entered a plea agreement for his involvement in the attempted poisoning and assassination of Frank Chikane, a prominent anti-apartheid leader. Vlok had previously applied for amnesty before the TRC for his role in three incidents: the bombing of Khotso House[226] in Johannesburg in August 1988, for which the activist Shirley Gunn was subsequently framed; the bombing of COSATU House[227] in Johannesburg in May 1987; and the use of explosives and bomb-scares in July 1988 to prevent the screening of *Cry Freedom*, a film about the death of Black Consciousness leader Steve Biko.

Vlok and his co-applicants were granted amnesty for each event by the TRC. Although the incidents in question caused physical harm and emotional trauma—a night watchman was injured in the Khotso House bombing, and Shirley Gunn was falsely imprisoned for two months without trial—their severity paled in comparison to other notable crimes of the apartheid regime. Indeed, in both the Khotso House and COSATU House amnesty decisions, the TRC noted the perpetrators' intent to avoid loss of life. Nevertheless, the limited extent of Vlok's disclosures was apparent to members of the Commission. Vlok testified that his knowledge and complicity only extended to two bombings and a few bomb scares. TRC Chair Archbishop Tutu rebuked Vlok for what he perceived to be a lack of candor: "We've not got all the answers we had wanted from you. This was our last chance to deal with our horrible past."[228]

Archbishop Tutu's statement, however, proved incorrect. In August 2006, Chikane, the former head of the South African Council of Churches and Vice-President of the UDF, made the surprising announcement that he had been approached by Vlok, who had apologized for his role in an attempt on Chikane's life in April 1989. Vlok quoted scripture and washed Chikane's feet, actions that,

---

[225] Luxolo Tyali, "APLA Four Get Suspended Sentence for Killing Cop," *Daily Dispatch*, June 22, 2006, http://www.dispatch.co.za/2006/06/22/Easterncape/cop.html.

[226] Khotso House was the headquarters of the ecumenical South African Council of Churches.

[227] Headquarters of the Congress of South African Trade Unions ("COSATU House").

[228] Wally Mbhele, "The Semantic Battles of Adriaan Vlok," *Mail & Guardian*, Oct. 17, 1997, http://www.mg.co.za/articledirect.aspx?articleid=206152&area=%2farchives%2farchives__print_edition%2f.

at least to some, represented genuine expressions of remorse from a broken man.
To others, including former TRC Commissioner Dumisa Ntsebeza, it was "too
little too late."[229] It subsequently emerged that Vlok had also met and apologized
to the mothers and widows of the Mamelodi Ten, a group of young activists killed
by Vlakplaas agent Joe Mamasela in June 1986. In the latter case, however, Vlok
specifically denied any knowledge of the operation.

In July 2007, the NPA announced that Vlok, together with former Police
Special Branch commanding officer Johan van der Merwe and three lower-
ranking police officers attached to the Security Branch, Chris Smith, Gert Otto,
and Manie van Staden, had been charged with the attempted assassination of
Chikane. A court date was set for August 2007. NPA spokesman Panyaza Lesufi
noted that Vlok and van der Merwe were originally scheduled to stand trial
in 2004, but that the NPA postponed the trial until the amended prosecution
guidelines were in place.[230]

The decision to prosecute Vlok created a firestorm of opinion. Boraine
captured the mood of much of the country's civil society: "I hope Vlok and
van der Merwe use the opportunity to share with the country what they know
about all that happened in those really dreadful, dark days."[231] Chikane himself
echoed this sentiment: "I say if you had someone in your family missing, you
could not just forget about it. I am interested in knowing what happened to me
and others who were victims of apartheid agents."[232] Others were less hopeful.
Khulumani, the victims' support group, used the opportunity to condemn the
amended guidelines as "too lenient" and likely to provide "new opportunities
... for apartheid criminals to once again seek indemnity from prosecution."[233]
AfriForum, an Afrikaner interest group, spoke out to remind the NPA of ANC
actions that were not being investigated: "Not treating the ANC leaders in
the same manner will amount to selective morality and the violation of the
constitutional principle of equality in the eyes of the law."[234]

---

[229] Karyn Maughan, "Vlok's Foot-Washing Apology to Chikane Flayed," *Independent
Online*, Aug. 28, 2006, http://www.int.iol.co.za/index.php?set_id=1&click_id=13&art_
id=vn20060828025759545C709145.

[230] "Vlok Charged With Chikane Poisoning," *Cape Argus*, July 17, 2007, http://allafrica.com/
stories/200707170754.html.

[231] *Ibid.*

[232] Ernest Mabuza, "South Africa: Chikane Forgives Vlok, But Says Prosecution is Separate
Matter," *Business Day*, July 18, 2007, http://allafrica.com/stories/200707181210.html.

[233] "Theatre of Differences Outside Vlok Trial," *Mail & Guardian*, Aug. 16, 2007, http://www.
mg.co.za/articlePage.aspx?articleid=316743&area=/breaking_news/breaking_news__na-
tional/.

[234] Kallie Kriel, "AfriForum Asks ANC Leaders to Follow Vlok's Example By Fully Disclos-

On August 17, 2007, with the country braced in anticipation of a high-ranking apartheid leader's trial, Vlok and his co-accused pleaded guilty to the attempted murder of Chikane. In exchange, a second charge of conspiring with Dr. Basson and others to kill Chikane was withdrawn. Although the co-accused initially sought amnesty under the amended guidelines, the plea agreement was concluded under Section 105A of the Criminal Procedure Act because, according to NDPP Pikoli, the co-accused had failed to disclose the full truth as required under the amended policy.[235]

In the plea arrangement, the parties agreed as a factual matter that the accused had "unlawfully and intentionally, in furtherance of a common purpose, attempted to murder the Reverend Frank Chikane."[236] The agreement, approved by the Pretoria High Court, called for prison sentences of ten years for Vlok and van der Merwe, and five years for the three police officers involved. In each case, the sentences were suspended for ten and five years, respectively. In addition, all five accused agreed to act as State witnesses in a possible future case against General Sebastiaan "Basie" Smit.[237] The NPA prosecutor responsible for the case, Anton Ackermann, said the case was not about retribution or revenge, but rather about reconciliation.[238]

The plea agreement generated fierce disagreements amongst South Africans on a number of fronts, ranging from whether a plea agreement was appropriate at all, to whether the NPA had obtained enough information in exchange for the plea, to whether the interests of the victim had been adequately protected. To many observers, including former TRC Commissioner Yasmin Sooka, the fact that such an arrangement was even an available option was wholly unacceptable: "Legal experts are saying technically, in terms of the Constitution and the NPA Act, plea bargains are a perfectly legitimate way of doing things. Yes, maybe a normal plea bargain in a normal criminal justice system. But when you're talking about political crimes, or crimes against humanity, then I think there are different questions that need to be asked. The [TRC] amnesty was done at a very special moment in history and should never

---

ing Their Own Atrocities of the Past," AfriForum Press Release, Aug. 13, 2007, http://www.afriforum.co.za/english?p=34.

[235] *Thembisile Nkadimeng and Others v. National Director of Public Prosecutions and Others*, High Court of South Africa (Transvaal Provincial Division), Case No. 32709/07, Affidavit of Achmed Mayat, May 21, 2008, para. 7.2 (quoting Affidavit of Vusi Pikoli).

[236] *In the Matter between the State and Johan van der Merwe et al.*, High Court of South Africa (Transvaal Provincial Division), Plea and Sentence Agreement, Aug. 17, 2007, para. 49.

[237] *Ibid.*, para.81.

[238] "All Smiles as Vlok, Chikane Bury Past," *Cape Times*, Aug. 18, 2007, http://www.capetimes.co.za/index.php?fSectionId=3531&fArticleId=vn20070818092151109C834686.

be repeated again."[239]

Chikane's involvement (or non-involvement) in the process also split opinion. One NPA prosecutor with knowledge of the case asserted that prosecutors were in contact with Chikane from the moment Vlok and his co-defendants decided to come forward, and that Chikane was involved throughout the entire process of negotiating the Vlok plea.[240] Despite Chikane initially making some favorable public comments about the plea arrangement, this picture was complicated by his revelation in May 2008 that he wrote a letter to the Justice Minister to complain about the NDPP's handling of the case. According to Chikane, he was not shown the plea bargain with Vlok in advance, he would never have agreed to suspended sentences for the accused, and he was surprised to hear in court that he had accepted the plea's terms. Chikane further characterized his interactions with the NDPP as "hostile, painful, and degrading" and stated that the NPA should be more concerned about the interests of victims.[241]

The agreement, however, did reveal previously unknown details of the attempt on Chikane's life. In 1987, Vlok and van der Merwe, along with other high-ranking members of the SADF, compiled a hit list that included Chikane. In 1989, General Smit, then head of the Security Branch, put three police officers in touch with Dr. Basson, leader of Project Coast, South Africa's secret chemical and biological weapons program. A potent poison was applied to Chikane's clothing as he left South Africa to lobby for economic sanctions against the government. Chikane fell violently ill in Namibia and the United States, but survived.

Commentators disagree on whether the information revealed by Vlok and his co-accused was sufficient to justify a plea. Former TRC Researcher Madeleine Fullard expressed the view that the case was notable because new information emerged: "We would never have known about the involvement of the Minister of Police and the Head of the Security Police and the police involved in the case if it hadn't been for the guidelines. They came forward on their own volition. . . . For me, that case was really important, about taking the notion of approving of violations right to the highest level of the State, which was something we could never do at the TRC. We could never take it above regional security police headquarters or the security police head office.

---

[239] International Human Rights Clinic interview with Yasmin Sooka, Former TRC Commissioner, Attorney, Executive Director of the Foundation for Human Rights, Pretoria, South Africa, Mar. 26, 2008.

[240] International Human Rights Clinic interview with NPA Prosecutor (name withheld), Pretoria, South Africa, Mar. 26, 2008.

[241] "Chikane was Unhappy about Vlok Deal, Inquiry Hears," S.A. Press Ass'n, May 7, 2008, http://www.citizen.co.za/index/article.aspx?pDesc=64735,1,22.

That case did it."[242] Moreover, as Chikane initially explained his own feelings of closure, "I'm pleased that I know what happened and that is where it ends."[243]

However, Graeme Simpson, of the International Center for Transitional Justice, provides a scathing commentary about the lack of full disclosure and the inability to procure guarantees of testimony against other perpetrators. Simpson starts:

> What is most striking are the terms of the plea bargain
> arrangement itself and the acknowledgements contained in it,
> which reveal information that was never even established by
> the TRC. In it, there is an explicit reference to orders being
> given for the "removal" of key opponents of apartheid but,
> of course, there is no specific detail of where these orders
> emanated from. So there's no disclosure of who the order-
> giver was but there's a clear reference to an order. There's
> also a reference to a "hit list", clearly indicating that Frank
> Chikane was not the only victim, but once again there's no
> disclosure of who else was on that hit list. And probably the
> most extraordinary acknowledgement was in the reference to
> Vlok—I'm not sure if it was in his role on the Cabinet or on
> the State Security Council—saying that in the ordinary course
> of events if one of these especially dangerous individuals was
> going to be eliminated, they would have been informed of
> it at the highest levels. But of course he suggests that in this
> particular case, he wasn't informed. The whole plea bargain
> flatters to deceive. Vlok seems to be taking responsibility for
> the attempt on Chikane's life but actually implies that he was
> not specifically informed, as was usually the case. So what we
> are left with is a remarkable set of acknowledgements which
> all fail to disclose any concrete information: you have an order,
> a hit list and an acknowledgment of a Cabinet or State Security
> Council-level protocol about taking out opponents and yet we
> have no real disclosure of details about any of them. If this
> was operating under the new prosecution procedures, then it

---

[242] International Human Rights Clinic interview with Madeleine Fullard, Former TRC Researcher, National Prosecuting Authority Missing Persons Task Team, Pretoria, South Africa, Mar. 26, 2008.

[243] "I'm Pleased that I Know What Happened," *Independent Online*, Aug. 17, 2007, http://www.int.iol.co.za/index.php?set_id=1&click_id=13&art_id=nw20070817121754437C571810.

offers a classic illustration of how this offers no guarantees of
further disclosures.[244]

In addition, if Vlok's plea agreement was intended to serve as a basis
for future prosecutions, Simpson's critique suggests that the disclosures were
inadequate for that purpose. The agreement notes generally that assassination
was an acceptable option for the government in extreme cases, and sets forth
specifically that at a 1987 meeting General van der Merwe was told of an order
"to act against high profile members of the anti-apartheid liberation struggle in
order to neutralize their influence."[245] The agreement does not disclose either the
origin of the order nor the other parties present at the meeting—information that
would be essential to pursuing prosecutions up the chain of command. The plea
agreement notes that Chikane's name was on a hit list, but Vlok did not publicly
disclose other names on the list. Further, the agreement considers Vlok's stated
lack of knowledge of the specific attempt on Chikane's life to be a mitigating
factor, despite Vlok's order that he be briefed on such attempts. The terms of the
plea leave unclear whether Vlok's command constituted an official government
protocol or his personal desire to remain informed of the special unit's progress.

Moreover, to date no charges have been brought against Smit, and Vlok
and his co-accused have made clear their reluctance to testify should Smit ever
be prosecuted. On the day the plea agreement was reached, they released a joint
statement declaring, "During the episode in question, General Smit had very
recently taken over command of the security branch. He found himself in an
unfamiliar environment and culture and would have experienced difficulty in
distinguishing between lawful powers and powers that, during the prevailing
abnormal circumstances in the country, were emphatically or tacitly implied by
a higher authority."[246] In addition to signaling their unwillingness to testify in
future cases, the five asserted that the bitterness of the past persists and that the
divide between various communities is ever-increasing: "Any person who does
not recognise this is living in a fool's paradise and has lost touch with reality."[247]
The solution they proposed was to "apply the same requirements to qualify for

---

[244] International Human Rights Clinic interview with Graeme Simpson, Attorney, International Center for Transitional Justice, Cape Town, South Africa, Mar. 31, 2008.

[245] *In the Matter between the State and Johan van der Merwe et al.*, Plea and Sentence Agreement, para. 36.

[246] Zelda Venter and Graeme Hosken, "Could Smit Be Next in Line?", *Pretoria News*, Aug. 18, 2007, http://www.iol.co.za/index.php?set_id=1&click_id=15&art_id=vn20070818092344345C265910.

[247] Gershwin Wanneburg, "Adriaan Vlok Spared Jail," *Mail & Guardian Online*, Aug. 17, 2007, http://www.mg.co.za/article/2007-08-17-adriaan-vlok-spared-jail.

amnesty that are applicable to members of the ANC and other organisations to ex-members of the security forces. Then come to an agreement that members of the national executive committee of the ANC and other political leaders will not be prosecuted in respect of incidents where amnesty has already been granted to other members of the ANC or other organisations."[248]

As with Vlok's appearance before the TRC in 1998, civil society and victims maintain that Vlok's plea agreement failed to reveal the full extent of his knowledge and information. For example, in explaining Vlok's displays of remorse as a mitigating circumstance, the plea refers to his visit to the mothers and widows of the Mamelodi Ten: "The sincere remorse of [Vlok] in regard to past deeds is further illustrated by his act of reconciliation towards the mothers of nine of the ten Nietverdiend victims killed by the Security Forces, despite the fact that [he] had no knowledge of this operation at the time and nor was it sanctioned by him."[249] In 2006, Vlok issued a similar public denial with respect to police hit squads operating out of Vlakplaas. To many, these denials ring hollow given Vlok's admitted visits to Vlakplaas, his concession that he used terms such as "eliminate" and "neutralize" to describe actions to be taken against activists,[250] and perhaps most importantly his position as Minister of Law and Order during the height of the repression. Vlok has asserted that he has nothing to say about the involvement of those higher up the chain of command, including F.W. de Klerk.[251] This stands in marked contrast to Eugene de Kock, who testified extensively before the TRC and continues to maintain that both F.W. de Klerk and P.W. Botha were intimately involved in Vlakplaas's activities, but who remains imprisoned for crimes he committed under Vlok's command. Van de Merwe, while acknowledging that there are many former senior government minister and leaders "who have knowledge of exactly what went on and who did what and under whose orders these crimes were committed," and who were "well aware of gross human rights violations committed by the foot soldiers," has declined to disclose any additional details.[252] Rather, he has noted that, "These people have

---

[248] *Ibid.*

[249] *In the Matter between the State and Johan van der Merwe et al.*, Plea and Sentence Agreement, para. 70.

[250] Yolandi Groenewald and Tumi Makgetla, "Vlok: 'My Role in Dirty War,'" *Mail & Guardian*, Sept. 8, 2006, http://www.mg.co.za/articlePage.aspx?articleid=283479&area=/insight/insight__national/.

[251] Prega Govender, "Vlok not completely off the hook," *The Times*, Aug. 19, 2007, http://www.thetimes.co.za/PrintEdition/News/Article.aspx?id=542795.

[252] Zelda Venter and Graeme Hosken, "Could Smit Be Next in Line?", *Pretoria News*, Aug. 18, 2007, http://www.iol.co.za/index.php?set_id=1&click_id=15&art_id=vn20070818092344345C265910.

failed to protect the security forces that, for over half a century, have protected them" by "leaving them out to dry by not accepting responsibility for their knowledge of what happened."[253]

In short, the incompleteness of the information brought to public light by the plea raises concerns about the ability of such agreements to reveal previously unknown facts and serve as a basis for further prosecutions. Simpson concludes that, "In the ordinary course of plea bargains, the accused usually trades with information about 'bigger fish', which of course is the real interest of the prosecution and makes for dramatic evidence by State's witnesses. The problem here is the obvious failed drama of Vlok actually trading information to ostensibly bust Basie Smit, a police commissioner who was in fact junior to Vlok as Minister of Police!"[254]

III. Persistent Debates, Inadequate Solutions

I think it was absolutely clear that the TRC regarded the anti-apartheid struggle as a just cause and a just war, and it regarded apartheid and the National Party government as unjust perpetrators of a crime against humanity in the form of apartheid. But then, what became a cause for a lot of debate was whether the TRC was evenhanded in its treatment of people from either side. I feel that even though one is fighting a just cause, one should still be held accountable for things that were done incorrectly, without a mandate, in the heat of the moment—things that were disproportionate in the way that they were carried out. . . . The ANC was certainly on the side of the good, but you had to look at excesses even within that good. If they were not so defensive about it, they would be able to show that they generally conducted one of the most principled and correct liberation struggles [of the twentieth century].

Jonathan Shapiro
Political Cartoonist
Cape Town, January 2007

You must understand that South Africa is not like other countries; it's a diverse country with so many nationalities. The minute you prosecute a white person, the white people say, "Well what about that black liberation movement leader

---

[253] *Ibid.*

[254] International Human Rights Clinic interview with Graeme Simpson, Attorney, International-al Center for Transitional Justice, Cape Town, South Africa, Mar. 31, 2008.

who did not apply for amnesty?" You understand? And the minute you take him on, [others] will say, "What about that white security . . . boss, who was never prosecuted?" So we need to balance those things . . . . There has to be an element of transparency in whatever we are doing so that at the end of the day we are not accused of covering things up. And there should be consistency in the manner in which we are handling those cases.

Anonymous
NPA Prosecutor
Pretoria, March 2008

The flawed implementation of the NPA's prosecutions policy is a reminder of the variety of complex factors at work behind these cases. Some speculate that the NPA has been largely unable to pursue apartheid-era cases because deal-making between ANC and NP leaders at the time of the negotiated settlement ensured that evidence would never be revealed, or because cases against high-level officials would lead to retribution and the revelation of secrets that could undermine the legitimacy of the ANC government. As Dumisa Ntzebeza notes, "There may well be, from our hideous past, people who are high in government who are compromised by associations which they had clandestinely with South African security forces."[255] Others assert that prosecutions have been delayed not because of insufficient commitment by NPA advocates, but rather because the NPA lacks the resources and skills necessary to pursue complex cases from the past. Still other critics charge that the NPA has not moved forward with prosecutions because of concerns about the consequences of losing such cases, and the implications that acquittals might have for the rule of law.

The pleas and trials that have occurred offer an opportunity to consider the meaning and value of evenhandedness and the role of moral relativism. Early trials demonstrate the dilemma of pursuing high-ranking officials versus foot soldiers, while the Vlok and APLA Four cases squarely present the question of whether prosecutions should involve both sides of the apartheid struggle. Prosecutions in South Africa have taken place under the gaze of society's aspirations and ideological, political, and racial differences, which means that evenhandedness carries different meanings for different people. To David Steward, Executive Director of the de Klerk Foundation,

---

[255] International Human Rights Clinic Interview with Dumisa Ntsebeza, Former TRC Commissioner, Advocate, Cape Town, South Africa, April 2008.

being evenhanded requires prosecuting both those on the liberation and the former apartheid government side in equal numbers: "If they decide to go ahead with prosecutions, they must be evenhanded. There must be equal protection and benefit. It is unacceptable to apply different standards."[256] To Former TRC Researcher Madeleine Fullard, evenhandedness means that moral nuances are relevant and that members of the liberation movements should be spared because they were fighting a just war against the apartheid State. Hugo van der Merwe and Audrey Chapman contend that "[i]nvestigations and prosecutions of perpetrators of human rights abuses had been overly focused on liberation forces in the past, while there is very little indication that state perpetrators have much to fear from the present state."[257] To Dumisa Ntsebeza, evenhandedness is akin to proportionality, meaning it is not just a question of numbers but rather of ensuring that prosecutions reflect the quantity and quality of crimes committed on all sides and the historical context. He argues that because the State was responsible for the majority of gross violations committed during the struggle, it should be the focus of the majority of the prosecutions. Evenhandedness could alternatively mean the system focuses on those at the highest levels who gave orders and set policy, and therefore bear the greatest responsibility, rather than on the foot soldiers who may have pulled a trigger but were given orders to do so.

In the end, however, issues such as evenhandedness remain largely unresolved because the implementation of the NPA's prosecutions policy has been decidedly sparse. Despite the limited number of prosecutions, however, they have had a lasting effect. The specter of the Basson case and of losing another high-profile trial remains, and the lack of prosecutorial vigor has been particularly pronounced since the loss. Since 2006, a new phenomenon—plea bargains—has also emerged and appears to now occupy the NPA's thinking; the lasting effects of the Vlok plea bargain are yet to be seen.

In addition, it is apparent that prosecutorial policy has been characterized by ad hoc implementation and a lack of established parameters for decision-making over the years. This contrasts sharply with the TRC process, with its statutory framework and established committees and

---

[256] International Human Rights Clinic interview with David Steward, Executive Director of the de Klerk Foundation, Cape Town, South Africa, Oct. 2006.

[257] Hugo van der Merwe and Audrey Chapman, eds., *Truth and Reconciliation in South Africa: Did the TRC Deliver?* (Philadelphia: University of Pennsylvania Press, 2008), p. 268. Jeremy Sarkin states, "More than half of the total amnesty applicants, and 80% of those who applied by December 1996, were in prison at the time of their applications. . . . Eventually, of more than 7,000 people who applied for amnesty, only about 2,500 of them actually applied for politically motivated crimes." Sarkin, p. 373.

procedures. This incoherence in prosecutorial policy has left open persistent debates about critical broad policy questions as well as the treatment of individual cases, such as the Vlok plea. Moreover, opportunities for public engagement have been missed. Media coverage of the APLA Four's plea agreement was notably absent. In the context of South Africa's ongoing attempt to address its painful past, this lack of publicity foreclosed public discussion about the implementation of prosecution policy, and silenced a dialogue that could have informed the proceedings against Vlok.

The Reflections that follow this chapter engage in wide-ranging and thought-provoking discussions—continuing the debate over evenhandedness, truth-telling, and the rights of victims when measured against competing social needs. They also dramatically present contrasting perspectives about the Vlok case as well as the overtly politicized nature of the current state of prosecutorial decision-making. Jan Wagener, for example, posits: "The answers here are not for lawyers because the problems cannot be solved by lawyers. It calls for a political solution." He also believes prosecutions will undermine long term stability. Dumisa Ntsebeza believes just the opposite: that the Vlok plea bargain negates "everything that the TRC tried to create as a standard for the future behavior of people in our society. . . . [The agreement is] the biggest way of making a reversal of the gains that began with the institution of the TRC." Pumla Gobodo-Madikizela views the Vlok case "as a deal to appease the senior members, the echelons of power[,]" but is just as troubled by the lack of imaginative thinking to come up with broad "solutions."

REFLECTION

"Prosecutions will take the country backward."

Jan Wagener, Attorney
Pretoria, October 2006

I was 42 years old when government changed in 1994. This was impossible for me. In a sense, I was the enemy because I had always represented the enemy. I grew up as a typical Afrikaner. By the late 1980s, it was evident that there had to be changes in the government. There were many different possible models; amnesty was only one of the choices on the table. When Namibia became independent in 1990, a general amnesty was granted for everyone. I was for this move in South Africa, and I advised for a general amnesty. It is short, brutal, and cruel, but that is the [most efficient] way.

But in South Africa it worked differently. In 1990, the politicians got together for the first time—the ANC and government. In 1990, there was the Indemnity Act. Under this Act, the State President could grant an indemnity to a specific person if he applied for indemnity for a specific incident; secondly, the State President could give a general indemnity to a category of people, which would then be published in the State Gazette and be law; thirdly, the State President could give a temporary indemnity to someone for a year at a time. Indemnity was granted under the third category to the ANC members. In 1992, there was the Further Indemnity Act. This made it easier to apply for indemnity. During this time period, no one in the State structures applied for the indemnity. It was a one-sided process: the liberation movements all applied for indemnity.[258]

The old police force was unified under one man, General van der Merwe. He asked me for advice regarding amnesty under the TRC. I advised him that the police should seek amnesties. This was a big step because the Amnesty Committee appeared to be a hostile environment [for applicants]. A lot of what the police had done was understandable [at the time] but unlawful. My influence led to a lot of ex-police officers coming into the amnesty process. The military, on the other hand, were divided on this issue because they lacked a single strong leader. They had more protection due to the rules of military law. The military

---

[258] For further explanation of the Indemnity Acts, see Dullah Omar, "Opening Address at Conference on Truth and Reconciliation," July 29, 1994, http://www.gov.za/search97cgi/ s97_cgi?action=View&Collection=Speech95&QueryZip=Nelson+Mandela%2Cinaugural& SortSpec=Score+Desc&SortOrder=desc&SortField=TDEDate&DocOffset=40&AdminScri ptName=&ServerKey=&AdminImagePath=%Fsearch97admimg%2F.

therefore decided to stay outside of the TRC process.

During the time the TRC was operating, my client base consisted of policemen and foot soldiers. The amnesty process focused on specific incidents. There was no amnesty in a general sense. This is difficult for senior [military] leaders who may not know about specific incidents. I concentrated on the command structures when making arguments for amnesty. Amnesty for the foot soldiers follows easily if amnesty is granted for the big wigs, if you follow the command structure. So the foot soldiers were in a better position [to gain amnesty] than the senior command because [the commanders] may have given instructions that led to outcomes they were unaware of. This was a problem on both the ANC [side] and my side. After the process had finished people in high positions were still at risk of prosecution. In my opinion, the TRC failed on the amnesty issue.

Regarding prosecution resulting from the political conflict of the past, I maintain that only three alternatives exist, namely: (a) prosecute each and every living person who is legally at risk; (b) prosecute nobody at all and thereby close the books of the past; (c) prosecute on a selective basis and only in a limited number of cases. To follow the first alternative would mean that for years to come our country will sit with many lengthy and highly emotional court cases, taking us back to previous decades and thereby destroying the little progress we have made on the road to building a young democracy on the foundation of peace, co-operation, and looking to the future. This option would mean that a number of high-ranking people presently in government structures, even including the cabinet and the State President, may find themselves standing accused. I am of the opinion that this will not serve the interest of our country and the public at large.

The third alternative should also not be implemented as questions will immediately arise, for example: Who will we prosecute if we don't prosecute everyone? Will all the names be put in four hats—SADF, SAP, ANC, PAC—and names then be drawn? Who will draw the names? How many names from each hat? Is it a case of bad luck if your name is drawn, and good luck if not? If we pick people as tokens, that would be wrong. There must be equality before the law. Surely this process can be seen as immoral and in conflict with the constitutional principle regarding equality before the law.

That leaves us with the second alternative, which I still say should be implemented. I realize the harshness [of this option] and even brutal cruelty towards victims and that arguments such as not applying for or being refused amnesty by the TRC will surely arise. On the other hand, it will be in line with what was negotiated at Kempton Park[259] and embodied in the epilogue to the Interim Constitution of 1993, namely that amnesty shall be granted for acts committed during the political conflict of the past. A number of individuals will no doubt be aggrieved, but it is part of the price a country has to pay for moving out of a war situation towards peace when the interest of the country unfortunately weigh heavier than those of certain individuals on all sides of the conflict. The answers here are not for lawyers because the problems cannot be solved by lawyers. It calls for a political solution.

Those who took part in the TRC process went through huge traumas; why should those people who did not take part in it get the benefit of an amnesty? It is a slap in the face. It is a hugely unfair process that those who went before the committee bared their souls. It was a very painful process. But it is better for the country in the long run if a general amnesty is now granted. There have been other benefits for victims including the taxes paid by whites, affirmative action, and Black Economic Empowerment. Prosecutions should be put to bed now, and a general amnesty should take effect. The people of South Africa would be trading peace and reconciliation for the future if they started prosecuting now. The option to unite people would be lost.

It would not be a win to have Mbeki in one cell and P.W. Botha in another. It would divide the country along black and white lines. South Africa is a violent country. It is hugely violent. Violence arises just like that. It is a sad reality. In some ways it is the legacy of the struggle: for generations, people were encouraged to break the law and make the country ungovernable. Now we're trying to change the inherent ethos of the nation from law-breaking to law-abiding. For a small number of people prosecutions would be wonderful, but not for the country itself. To make real progress over the long-term, we have to ascend above that individual agony. There are conflicting fundamental rights, but in striking a balance we have to look at the big picture.

The wounds were raw in 1994. To some extent they still are today. I'm optimistic South Africa is going the right way, but South Africa has not come far yet. There are huge distances to cover and mountains to climb. We have barely departed on that voyage.

---

[259] Kempton Park, site of the Johannesburg World Trade Centre, is where multiparty negotiations known as the Convention for a Democratic South Africa (CODESA) took place between the government and liberation movements between 1991 and 1993.

REFLECTION

"We can't prosecute everybody . . .
[but] we can't not prosecute anyone."

Dumisa Ntsebeza , Former TRC Commissioner, Advocate
Cape Town, April 2008

The clear recommendation of the TRC was that those people who had either applied for but were denied amnesty because they didn't comply with the requirements, particularly the requirements of full disclosure, or those people who had not come to the TRC, would be prosecuted. So that was our expectation. But those cases have been very few and far between. The whole ethos of the liberation struggle was to produce a society that would be transparent, open, accountable, and government has not done that. I have not, speaking for myself, found a clear or satisfactory reason why there haven't been more prosecutions.

Why hasn't more of an effort been made? There are kind and unkind answers that I could give. If I want to be kind, I will say that there are constraints, capacity constraints. We continually hear that there are not very many qualified prosecutors. The prosecutorial services in this country have been pretty much uniracial and unisexual for a long time. So it's been totally untransformed, and that continues to be a view that is prevalent in our in society. The unkind explanation is that there is no political will. There may well be, from our hideous past, people who are high in government who are compromised by associations which they had clandestinely with South African security forces. People would rather bury and try and forget the past. But unfortunately, it won't [go away].

Prosecutions in and of themselves will not reveal all the truth, because prosecutions have never been a good mechanism to expose the truth. You expose the truth, which is contested, only to the extent that you may be able to prove beyond a reasonable doubt that what you present is the truth. But whether it is in fact [the truth] is something else. To that extent, prosecutions will be what prosecutions the world over have been: a vengeful act on the part of the State seeking to bring the criminals to book. Will prosecutions be of any solace to the victims? They will only bring about any peace-of-mind to the victims if, for instance, over and above being proved criminally guilty the perpetrators also accept and acknowledge the crimes that they committed. In the case of disappearances, [perpetrators] should make efforts to reveal how and where the people disappeared. If that isn't achieved, then only one purpose of prosecutions will have been served: society will feel that the guilty have had their comeuppance. Is that justice? Well, I don't know.

We can't prosecute everybody. It's impossible. Even if it were possible, I don't think it's desirable. That having been said, we can't *not* prosecute anyone. And I disagree with de Klerk and his foundation when he says that if you prosecute an Adriaan Vlok today, the next day you must prosecute a Thabo Mbeki. That is rubbish because it's not evenhanded. The evidence that we have—which is uncontroverted even by the National Party who participated in the TRC process—the evidence the TRC was able to produce is that out of every ten cases of gross violations of human rights, nine out of those cases were committed by apartheid-era security forces. So that ratio must be respected. To be evenhanded you would have to prosecute nine of the apartheid-era security forces for each one of the liberation forces. I'm not even saying there must be that sort of sequential arrangement of prosecutions. But we can't begin to cry foul simply because today and tomorrow and the next day we have got a line-up of what are quite clearly security forces criminals who are in for prosecutions. The evidence is there to show the degree and the extent of their involvement in gross violations of human rights in the requisite period.

I think that's where the question of political will becomes an issue. And you say to yourself, why are these people dithering? Why is it possible for de Klerk and some of the apartheid-era security forces, after one prosecution has been mounted, to be able to succeed in warding off any attempts at prosecutions simply by saying there is no evenhandedness, people are being targeted?

The Vlok plea was a bloody ruse. I mean, our intelligence was insulted. Here I am not unbiased because I have taken to task both Vlok and Revered Chikane. I think [Chikane] was also complicit in some ways in trying to let the fact that his feet were washed and the fact that he was prepared to forgive override the critical importance of what was the cornerstone of the amnesty provisions in the [TRC] Act. I don't think anybody has got any quarrels about [Vlok] not going to jail necessarily, because he has got a criminal record now, he admitted things. But I think some of us are militating against those guidelines for the very reason that there is no transparency, there is no process that involves victims in the way in which the amnesty provisions involved victims.

With Chikane, he will say he was involved. But some of the things that are in that plea bargain to which he agreed are outrageous. He is made to say that he understands that there was this war of low-intensity, which is incomprehensible. Because where is Vlok? It's not as though he never came to the TRC. He came to the TRC, but only for the bombing of Khotso House. And now, so many years after the TRC has closed, he comes again. Now, if you ask me, who dealt with him in that period of the state of emergency, when he personally was going into all the townships in the Hippos, he can't say he was not aware of the levels of atrocities that were meted out to the ordinary people by his security forces under his command. And under the international doctrine of command responsibility he must take the blame for what has happened. But I go so far as to say he was intimately aware. He can't plead ignorance.

In 1997, we called [Vlok] as head of the security forces, we called the ANC, the PAC, the police, the intelligence services, and we had a hearing. And at that hearing we specifically put to him some of the things that came out of the State Security Council minutes where they had taken decisions that, for instance, the leaders of the UDF must be eliminated. He prevaricated about the meaning of elimination, and he told us that elimination in that context meant that they must be permanently detained, as though there were no words that could have been used to say that! And in any case the brigadiers were saying, "We understood that very clearly to mean we must kill the people." And I put it to him, I said, "What then did you do when people were not just detained, they were murdered? The Cradock Four. These people were murdered! What did you do?" Far from making sure that justice was brought there, he said, "We ordered an inquest." And I said, "And what did your people say?" Don't tell me that he didn't realize that these people were lying, and that he was part of that lie.

The point I'm making is: are you prepared to make a full disclosure as was required? Because that's the whole aim and purpose of what the TRC was about. In order for complete healing to take place, those who were perpetrators must be prepared to acknowledge their wrongdoings, to come out openly so that it leaves room for victims to say, "It is still painful for us to know what happened but at least now we know." And then we can get to a point where we can really console ourselves to the reality that this man, this woman, who is a monster [given] a description of the things that he or she was up to, nonetheless has owned up and asked for forgiveness and is still a member of society. We have to live with him or her.

The notions of restorative justice nowadays insist that it will also be justice if the criminal not only repents and becomes contrite but, after an adequate punishment has been meted out, the criminal should be restored

as a useful member of society. Now, that is the process. It won't come with
a plea bargain that takes place in the dark recesses of one court, in a stage-
managed trial where you have only fifteen minutes from beginning to end.
It's a travesty of justice. It's an insult. It's an insult to the victims; it's an insult
to the entire TRC process. The Vlok plea bargain is a clear indication that
these prosecutorial guidelines are doomed to be a negation of everything that
the TRC tried to create as a standard for the future behavior of people in our
society. It's the biggest indictment you can make, the biggest way of making a
reversal of the gains that began with the institution of the TRC.

Reflection

"The Vlok plea: it wasn't a disclosure.
It was an apology to Frank Chikane."

Pumla Gobodo-Madikizela, Member,
TRC Human Rights Violations Committee, Psychologist, Professor
Cape Town, April 2008

I think the beauty of the TRC is that it embraced all of these processes: a process of reconciliation, or at least a process that encouraged reconciliation, a dialogue of reconciliation. At the same time, it allowed perpetrators an opportunity to reflect on what they did. That is something important as well. Here is a moment in our history where all actors are brought together—victims, perpetrators, bystanders. It creates a possibility for wonderful human moments, when perpetrators truly look back and regret what they did in a way they would never be able to in a court of law.

But the problem now is continuity, and how to structure continuity. The TRC has ended, but the need for the dialogue continues. There is so much more than needs to happen. We still haven't figured out how to have a national dialogue about the past. Sparks fly on radio airwaves, in national newspapers, angry voices of people from all sides. But what is disconcerting is when you hear so many voices of white people who were beneficiaries, of people who can't find a path within their hearts to really reflect on the past and see that they benefited from apartheid.

If voters had decided they were not voting for the system many years ago, we would not have had the problem of apartheid. There are white people who did not vote for apartheid, who opposed apartheid, but it's a minority by far. Those people, some of whom voted [for apartheid], it seems to me if I were to look at it psychologically, are reluctant to confront their role in the past. As a result, they slip into roles of denial and projection of anger. You know, "The power failures, it's the black government. The crime, it's the black government." Anything that is wrong is the black government. And as soon as they say that, black government then is transformed into black people. Then it feeds into old scripts and, as we've seen in the past year, elements of racism being reenacted in the public sphere. What to do about that? I don't think that prosecutions will necessarily restore a sense of peace, nor do I think they will address those subtleties in the transformation process. I don't think that prosecutions will necessarily, on their own, address those issues.

Again, I think it will be important to tread carefully there. The frustrating thing is that whenever there is talk about prosecutions, and there is an individual who has been identified and is being investigated, and if that person is a senior person, has a profile in the old apartheid era, such as Adriaan Vlok, there is a huge outcry. Then come questions about the ANC, "Why don't they prosecute the ANC?" There are all these defensive responses. So what happens then is that the NPA, at least in [Vlok's] case, it seems that the NPA just dropped the case. I mean it just fizzled out like that. I don't know what the actual conditions of this case were, but it was just so odd that one moment there was talk of prosecuting this man, and the next moment, literally the next moment, he was smiling and hugging Frank Chikane. It didn't seem to me that there was any clear indication of an honest attempt to prosecute this man. It seemed to me that there was a show. What this tells us is that this process of prosecutions is not simple. We may say, yes, let's pursue them, but it's not simple in a society like ours. It would be good, or commendable, if the complaints would be balanced with voices of apology, or if not apology then acknowledgement—because people may not know how to get to the point of apologizing, for whatever reason, but at least [they should] be able to say, "Gosh, yes, we benefited."

The Vlok plea: it wasn't a disclosure. It was an apology to Frank Chikane. I saw it as a deal to appease the senior members, the echelons of power. I think there was too much of an effort to appease that group of people at the expense of a process that would really have earned praise from society to be able, for once, to actually do something about the person who was in charge. One of the things that I have pondered—it's not a huge concern, but I've just pondered about—is that a person like Adriaan Vlok has to apologize not just to the victims of apartheid. He has to apologize to people like Eugene de Kock,[260] for example, who continues to languish in jail because of what he did under Vlok's command. He has to apologize to the many police who are out in the cold. They're not even campaigning for their presidential [pardon] applications.[261] So it's very complex, that issue of so-called disclosure. It wasn't

---

[260] Based on 47 interviews she conducted with de Kock from his prison cell, Gobodo-Madikizela wrote a book about evil and the psychology of forgiveness. *See A Human Being Died That Night* (New York: Houghton Mifflin, 2003).

[261] In November 2007, then-President Thabo Mbeki announced the formation of a multi-party Pardons Reference Group to solicit and consider applications for pardons for politically-motivated crimes committed before June 1999. Mbeki described the process as a way of addressing the unfinished business of the TRC. Unlike the TRC, however, the Pardons Reference Group was not asked to hear the testimony of victims, and its proceed-

disclosure.

It was just a deal, because this was a Minister for goodness sake. He was the Minister of Police for years, and to what extent did he tell us how these people [operated]? Eugene de Kock, for example, [Vlok] gave him the purple star, the highest award. Why did he give [it] to de Kock? If he has nothing to say about de Kock's actions, why would he have pinned the purple star on his uniform? It leaves so many unanswered questions. And the message that it sends is that there is a fear among the people who could make prosecutions work, fear on different levels, and uncertainty, and an attempt to keep the good spirit of reconciliation. It seems that there is so much that is known, but it appeared that the NPA either is too afraid to venture into this investigation or they are caught up in some Catch-22 situation. Sometimes I wonder if the investigators are afraid of touching fire. Some of these people are dangerous. And I suspect that there may be a fear of consequences, dire consequences.

Isn't it amazing, really, under the circumstances, that there is peace in this country, in spite of the crime? Isn't it amazing? The unfortunate thing is that some white people perceive crime as something that is targeting them as a way of getting back at whites, because the color of crime is black in this country. Little do they know, or they don't want to know. I work in Khayelitsha, I work in Gugulethu, and the levels of crime are unimaginable, and the kinds of crimes to the body of the person, you cannot imagine. And so it's really with sadness that there is a sense of entitlement among so many white people.

It is in the nature of transition in many countries, and there are reasons why things turn out this way. This is a generation of people who experienced violation and oppression. During apartheid, the language of violence was framed within the anti-apartheid struggle. That struggle is no longer in existence, so the anger and frustration has not gone away, in part because there hasn't been any real serious—apart from black empowerment strategies that tend to privilege only a few—or clear indication of what the strategy and thinking is around some form of reparations, restoring people's dignity, improving the quality of life. Instead, some people have lost their jobs, have come to the cities and found they really have no role to play in civil society, a sense of worthlessness in all of this.

---

ings were not to be public. Following interim President Kgalema Motlanthe's indication that he planned to go ahead with the process, a coalition of South African NGOs brought a case in March 2009 to challenge the constitutionality of the pardons process. In April 2009, the North Gauteng High Court issued an interim interdict preventing the president from issuing any pardons until the proceedings in the case are concluded.

The issue of economic justice if a very topical, even crucial one. In any form of truth commission, it is not enough to invite people to share their stories of pain. One must then think about what they've lost and how best to give them back their dignity. On the TRC, we talked about how this process restores dignity, it validates people's experiences, and acknowledgement makes them the centre of attention and all that. But people go home and then they face their losses all over again, particularly if the person who was killed or disappeared was the breadwinner. Even if they are not a breadwinner, just the sense of loss and how people's lives changed as a result of this loss. So a process of repairing that—this is what truth and reconciliation is about.

So the repairing must not only happen by granting perpetrators amnesty in exchange for truth. It must also repair the brokenness among victims, so many of whom lost irreparably. I think one of the most important things that needs to happen is a reparations strategy. We made proposals, which the government did not take seriously because they thought it was a lot of money. Money, of course, on its own will not cause people to start relating to one another in a reconciled manner. The way of repairing is really creating ways of helping people with education, at least the next generation, so that the children who were born at the time the victims were killed would at least be assured of a different life through education. It is people's sense of dignity that we are repairing.

The Truth Commission was very narrowly focused on specifics of what was defined as gross human rights violations. But now when it comes to repairing what was broken, repairing the destruction, then we have to think more broadly. I don't think that the people in leadership have exercised their minds enough to be imaginative enough to come up with solutions.

CHAPTER 5

Prosecutions: Reflecting Back, Moving Forward

"The only way you're going to find out what happened is if you get someone to come and disclose. . . . [D]o you think they're going to tell us in the context of a court case, where they're pleading innocent? They're not."

Madeleine Fullard, Former TRC Researcher, NPA Missing Persons Task Team
Pretoria, March 2008

The main drive [for the exhumations carried out by the NPA's Missing Persons Task Team] wasn't prosecutions, it was actually really more restitution, restorative justice. My view is that really there's been a deliberate lethargy and concern from government around opening the whole thing of prosecutions, even though it's implicit in the TRC contract that there would be such prosecutions. They've had a lot of threats and pressure from security forces and their lawyers, who have raised the idea that there must be evenhanded prosecutions. So, let's look at prosecutions. We've had, over the last 34 years, about 60,000 people detained without trial. We've had tens of thousands imprisoned. We've had 134 people, at least, hanged for political offences. We've had thousands of people placed under house arrest. So let's talk about evenhanded prosecutions. When shall the clock start? Because it's not starting now. So that's a very problematic notion, this notion that now the slate is clean.

A lot of NGO people tend to think that we're just going to prosecute the State. Unfortunately the law doesn't work that way, if you're going to go in for prosecutions. Unfortunately, because the state over time has been cumulatively compiling dockets. If you look at deaths, [there were] 25,000 deaths in South Africa between 1960 and 1994, roughly. Between 14,000 and 16,000 of those are inter-civilian deaths, ANC-IFP. Are we going to prosecute those? Those are ordinary civilians. A whole lot of the debate around prosecutions is predicated on a poor understanding of the nature of the political violence of the past. If you have Khulumani saying, "Yeah, we want prosecutions," do they understand it's going to possibly be their neighbor down the street who was involved in the street committee [who is prosecuted]? Because a docket will exist for that. A docket won't exist for the torture of some person. And the NPA can't in good faith decline to prosecute when there's viable evidence.

This is the problem with the law and the fantasies, to some extent, of the NGO community around the way that the law operates. You can't just decide, oh, well, you're not going to prosecute this case. And the fact that if mainly prosecutions are going to be around deaths, then there's this question of inter-civilian violence. There were about 800 to 1,000 people who were burnt and necklaced[262] to death during the political conflict, mainly by civilians, for which dockets exist and evidence exists. I also sort of come from that human rights world, that's very much about let's hold the State accountable. But I think there's a lack of really thinking through what it would mean in practice.

I also have a problem with the kind of notion of the human rights community, in that I feel it instrumentalizes victims to some extent, saying that, "Yes, prosecutions are going to bring you what you need, [bring you] an answer." In our experience, working with families of disappeared people, court processes are so remote from their worlds, utterly remote. Things that happen in a remote courtroom somewhere else mean very little. That's a problem which must be addressed.

The human rights community and the NGOs are very much pushing justice, and an end to impunity. But the victims that I spoke to, their first demand was, "We want to know what happened. We want the remains." Then you start asking, what about justice? "Yeah, yeah, okay." What does justice mean? "The same thing must be done to the perpetrator as he did to my

---

[262] Necklacing is a method of execution believed to have originated in the Eastern Cape in the 1980s. It refers to forcing a rubber tire over the victim's body, filling the tire with gasoline, and then setting it on fire, thus burning the victim to death. This method was often used on suspected informants or collaborators.

daughter or son." No mention of a court case. But the NGOs are all organizing the victims to demand justice. Of course the human rights people are opposed to amnesties. But in fact, especially for disappearances, amnesty holds out the best [chance of finding the truth]. I mean, some kind of amnesty process actually can offer something to families. So I find myself very torn between the kind of imperatives of the international human rights movement and its focus on ending impunity and justice, and what the families talk about. I'm not saying that justice is off their horizon or not important at all. Probably if they got the remains, their very next thing will be, "Charge the bastards!"

But I find that with missing persons, the debate tends to marginalize the issue of actually getting information, and remains in a context where you've got two kinds of burial situations. You've got situations where people are killed and the bodies are left lying around in the street or dump. Then you've got secret burials, where only the perpetrators know where they've put the people. We're not going to find them, even if we know that they're somehow on this particular farm. It's hectares, twenty years ago. Do you think we can spot it? There's no magic tool. So, in those cases, for us, the prospect of a plea bargain or a disclosure-based scenario [doesn't look so bad]. Because of the problems of the amnesty process, a lot of people didn't come who should have come, who maybe wanted to come. And this goes for the liberation movements too, because I think they will be the main beneficiaries of a disclosure-based program. People always think it's only going to benefit the security forces. But the people who it really is going to benefit are ordinary people who participated in street violence.

This whole Frank Chikane thing was much attacked and yes, there were problems with it. But we would never have known about the involvement of the Minister of Police and the Head of the Security Police and the police involved in the case if it hadn't been for the guidelines. And nobody must fantasize and say oh, we should have investigated. We hadn't a clue! No knowledge about that. They came forward on their own volition. I was like, "My God!" This was so shocking. I think people are inaccurate when they say, "How can you give such leniency and those suspended sentences?" For me, that case was really important, about taking the notion of approving of violations right to the highest level of the state. Which was something we could never do at the TRC. We could never take it above regional security police headquarters or the security police head office. We could never take it beyond. That case did it.

I don't think the newspapers in the country really grasped the significance of it. That's partly because the issue of prosecutions is pretty much dead in this country. Even though the human rights and NGO community likes to think otherwise, it's really not an issue that is burning. Otherwise we wouldn't have such problems. If the State had more of a sense of a public demand for these things, there would be less obstacle-making.

I think the State's anxieties around prosecutions are various. One, I said, is the pressure from security forces. Secondly, I think, there has been obviously a suspicion created. You can argue this conspiratorially or not. There's a perception created that the staff of the PCLU are old guard people who just want to prosecute the ANC. That's been deliberately created, I think by default. The irony is that it is actually only the people in the PCLU who have been really struggling to try and get some prosecutions going, against the wishes of everybody else. And I think there is anxiety at the State level about the consequences if there are prosecutions for the liberation movement too. Which is an absolutely legitimate issue. I think the guidelines emerged out of those concerns. I don't have problems with any of those [guidelines], actually. I'm actually quite in favor of an ongoing disclosure-based problem. Because prosecutions sure aren't going to bring any disclosure. Prosecutions are the antithesis of disclosure. They're all about denial and pleading innocent. So you can't say the families are going to get answers. The main thing that families asked when they came to the TRC—they didn't say we want justice—they said we want to know what happened. That was the thing. That was the main, number one, overwhelming demand.

That's really my ongoing issue. I do call myself a human rights person but, at the same time, I find that the agenda is very constructed by what's going on in international human rights circles. It very much reflects their insertion into an international setting, an insertion that wasn't there at the beginning of the Truth Commission process but is now there. Now people want to prescribe these internationally [approved procedures], which is legitimate and appropriate. But again, we have had a Truth Commission process, we have had an amnesty process. We've got a situation here that is not an Argentina where you can send all the generals to prison. [In South Africa] it's going to involve liberation movement people.

What do you really want? I don't know if Khulumani has really sat down and really grappled with that issue. Do they want some of their own members to face charges? It's very much cast as a political debate rather than really concrete thinking about what is this going to mean. What does it mean when many of Khulumani's members have missing family members and may benefit from a disclosure-based process? Partly I'm being devil's advocate. But I do think that there have to be interrogations of the kind of unilateral call for prosecutions without considering the particular context. I know some people say, "Well then, the liberation movements must just [face prosecutions]." Well, do you really think we're going to have a situation where half the cabinet is charged? I mean, is that going to happen, and is that appropriate, in a context where people actually did lay down their lives fighting against something that was a crime against humanity? I have a problem with that. I'm not an evenhandedness [believer], a violation is a violation [proponent]. I do see those kind of moral nuances as relevant.

Which puts me at odds, actually, with my colleagues, because they really think a murderer is a murderer is a murderer, and it doesn't matter who did it, they must be prosecuted. They're really just prosecutors, and bring the docket, and where's the evidence. That's the irony, that kind of suspicion from the government side that [the PCLU advocates] are political animals who have a hidden agenda. But actually, it's the complete opposite; they're just prosecutors who want to prosecute. The political agenda is actually at a government level. So there's a misreading going on there, I feel.

I find that [symbolic prosecutions of a few well know figures would be] quite harsh for the individuals. And I would have a real problem participating in a court process that selected those individuals. I don't know if I could live with myself. You're just saying, "Let's have a few sacrificial lambs." I can't be party to choosing those people. I would find that very difficult. And what's that about? Do you know how instrumental that is of victims as well? "Let's have prosecutions, but well, let's just have a few." That's dishonest.

I also get a sense that some of these human rights people [believe], "If we have prosecutions you might find the body." Forget it! The last thing you're going to find if we have prosecutions is the body. The only way you're going to find out what happened is if you get someone to come and disclose. Three years of doing missing persons work convinces me of that, absolutely. We are not going to find her body unless someone tells us. And do you think they're going to tell us in the context of a court case, where they're pleading innocent? They're not. So it's actually disingenuous and cruel to families to suggest [otherwise], and now to get them to be signatories to a big court case challenging [the guidelines]. I really have problems to it.

That family needs to decide what they want the most. If they want the remains, if that's what they really want, then a disclosure-based process is possibly the way for them. So they've been recruited into a human rights agenda around prosecutions, legitimately I feel at this point, because there aren't any prosecutions or plea bargains going on. If there was a dynamic process going on with lots of people coming in and making disclosures and getting information and doing exhumations based on those disclosures, [it would be different]. So in a sense I don't blame them. That's what the option is now.

I. INTRODUCTION

Madeleine Fullard's Reflection, along with the other South African voices and perspectives that fill these pages, depict the complexity associated with societies in transition as they wrestle with questions of truth, reconciliation, and accountability, including the place of prosecutions in efforts to move a country forward from a painful past. In seeking to obtain truth and achieve corrective justice along with restorative and distributive justice, the South African experience makes clear the importance of both the TRC and prosecutions: each is a critical piece in the larger transitional justice puzzle.

Ultimately, the lesson learned for other transitional societies is that the question of prosecutions is a core component of rebuilding a society and must be directly confronted, sooner or later, by policy-makers and leaders as well as communities, victims, and perpetrators. As South Africa demonstrates, for transitional justice initiatives to be effective they must be done well. This is equally true of truth commissions as of prosecutions, and is especially important when both processes are intended to complement each other to foster justice and reconciliation. In South Africa, however, more time, energy, and emotion has been dedicated to the TRC process than to prosecutions. In contrast to the prolonged and thoughtful public debate that led to the creation of the TRC and shaped its mandate, no similar national discussion has been conducted with respect to prosecutions of apartheid-era crimes. Many mistakenly viewed the TRC as *the* transitional process, rather than as a mechanism that initiated a prolonged transition composed of different initiatives and phases. As a result, there has been a sense of indecision—and ultimately inaction—around prosecutions, leaving many with a sense of dissatisfaction and uneasiness about the whole issue.

In the immediate aftermath of the end of apartheid, the TRC and prosecutions were inextricably linked. With the passage of time, however, the policy and implementation of prosecutions for apartheid-era crimes have drifted, relegated to apparent second-class status behind the TRC. Yet while the TRC achieved much, it left behind unfinished business on reparations as well as systemic issues such as poverty alleviation. This final chapter explores how the TRC's unfinished business and prosecutions could be productively linked once again. Indeed, as Jody Kollapen's closing Reflection discusses, a concerted and imaginative prosecutions policy may offer new opportunities to continue the transformative transition away from apartheid. By moving the discussion about prosecutions beyond a singular focus on trials and imprisonment, and by requiring that perpetrators do more than apologize or acknowledge their role, prosecutions could help address lingering inequities resulting from apartheid, hold individuals accountable, and move the country forward in ways that are mutually reinforcing and embrace the notion of *ubuntu*.

II. THE NEED FOR A COHERENT, CONTEXTUALIZED STRATEGY

South Africa's experience indicates that significant practical difficulties confront any country addressing widespread human rights violations. A single approach often will not suffice, as transitional societies will be forced to address many complex and overlapping problems—ones that are ever-changing over time. A government must thus adopt a coherent strategy that integrates different approaches to justice, while also taking into consideration evolving societal expectations. For example, without any truth-telling or reparations efforts, prosecutions of selected perpetrators may be perceived as victor's justice or simply revenge. Without prosecutions that hold individuals accountable, truth-telling may become mere words of little consequence. Without prosecutions and truth-telling, reparations may be seen as callous attempts to buy victims' silence.

In addition, any transitional justice strategy must take into account what a country can reasonably achieve at any given point in time. It may be more damaging to the rule of law and reconciliation to raise expectations that are not met than to set goals that are less than ideal but still attainable. Societies emerging from mass atrocity often lack strong, functioning judicial systems, and simply may not have the institutional or personnel capacity to prosecute numerous perpetrators. Alternatively, a nascent democracy may risk its stability and impede a transition if it pursues an ambitious prosecutions effort. When confronted with such political and practical difficulties, "the law cannot ignore this reality and must seek to encourage credible alternatives, rather than simply condemn, when punishment is realistically not possible. Otherwise, the law will be ignored and cease to encourage appropriate state conduct."[263] In South Africa, this imperative dictated that excruciatingly

---

[263] Paul van Zyl, "Justice Without Punishment: Guaranteeing Human Rights in Transitional

difficult compromises were made: in order to move the country from apartheid to majority rule, the outgoing government required assurances that it could receive amnesty for prior abuses. This compromise was accepted, although only when coupled with the requirement of full-disclosure of past crimes and the promise that those who did not receive amnesty would be prosecuted.

The attitude of society's members is also fundamental to shaping policy. Transparency, participation, and empowering processes that assess the needs of victims and ensure citizens are heard and incorporated into the transitional process are critical. This is especially important because victims are themselves not a monolithic group. Their needs may include legal justice, revenge, truth, apology, or simply a desire to forget the past, but these different hopes and expectations must be taken into account. Transitional justice strategies that reflect and incorporate a society's aspirations, and well as its limitations, stand the best chance of success.

III. THE POWER (AND LIMITS) OF PROSECUTIONS

Prosecutions are an essential component of an integrated response to widespread human rights abuses, and should be pursued wherever possible. Yet prosecutions are often narrowly associated, if not exclusively associated, with imprisonment and punishment. This focus on individual perpetrators and guilt may overly constrain thinking surrounding prosecutions policy. If creatively conceived and conducted, prosecutions could reveal the motivations and means for committing massive human rights violations, while also restoring both victims' dignity and public confidence in the rule of law.

Prosecutions can uphold the rule of law by preventing impunity and demonstrating to marginalized members of society that the legal system works for them. Although it is simply not feasible to prosecute every individual perpetrator, even selective prosecutions can reinvigorate confidence in the State's commitment to human rights and accountability, building a foundation for collective self-government while demonstrating compliance with international human rights obligations and standards. Prosecutions may also assist in breaking cycles of revenge and violence. For example, Yasmin Sooka has identified a nexus in South Africa between the crimes of the past and the rampant crime of the present, noting that impunity begets more impunity: "I think a lot of the violence in our country has to do with a sense

---

Societies," *Looking Back, Reaching Forward: Reflections on the Truth and Reconciliation Commission of South Africa* (Cape Town: University of Cape Town Press, 2000), p. 43.

of dispossession and alienation."[264] In a new democracy seeking to inculcate a deep-seated belief in the fundamental governing precepts of human rights and dignity, prosecutions may bolster confidence in the State's commitment to these values and demonstrate that the law can be applied in a manner that is impartial rather than politicized. While declining to prosecute those responsible for gross violations of human rights might imply forgiveness and reconciliation have been achieved, it could equally indicate persistent fear, a desire to forget the past, or simply a lack of political will.

Prosecutions also carry a powerful demonstrative effect: by securing justice for individual victims, a prosecutions regime can demonstrate the State's commitment to justice for all people, as well as to equal enforcement of and protection under the law. In contrast, a lack of prosecutions may signal that those in power still do not hear the voices of victims. Sooka points out that prosecutions targeted at high-level perpetrators, "will restore a sense of faith that the system works for us as well. That's part of what a transitional justice process is supposed to be about: the fact that ordinary citizens who were excluded from the protection of the State are enabled to feel that the institutions of State work for them. One of the problematic areas about South African cases is that many black people come away feeling that the judiciary still protects the old order. [Prosecutions are] what we need to do, to show ordinary people that we can restore faith and civic trust in government."[265]

Yet only some survivors would directly benefit from prosecutions and trials, since there are far more people who suffered than there is evidence or funding to pursue individual cases. Although a focus on selective prosecutions carries the risk of allowing those who were complicit to shirk their own collective responsibility, it still carries the potential benefit of offering an avenue away from cycles of blame that may lead to desires for revenge or tensions among different groups. Beyond punishing abuses or providing a deterrent effect, prosecutions can help establish an aura of fairness and a sense of accountability, demonstrating that no one is above the law. In the right circumstances, these goals could be achieved without solely relying on criminal proceedings and imprisonment. In addition to showing that the justice system can operate in an unbiased manner on behalf of even marginalized members of society, prosecutions may also begin a broader process of social, psychological, and material transformation, by stimulating dialogue about the continuing

---

[264] International Human Rights Clinic interview with Yasmin Sooka, Former TRC Commissioner, Attorney, Executive Director of the Foundation for Human Rights, Pretoria, South Africa, Mar. 26, 2008.
[265] *Ibid.*

need for reparations and reconciliation.

IV. THE POTENTIAL FOR TRANSFORMATION

I am saying that the punitive measure, the stick of prosecutions, is the driving force of other things, because from that could come disclosure, and from that could come reparations and other benefits to victims, both material and psychological.

Jonathan Shapiro
Political Cartoonist
Cape Town, January 2007

[In a municipality south of] Johannesburg, near where Sharpeville is located. . . . I went to a commemoration of people who had fought against apartheid. One of the people being honoured, who was once on death row, said that she was so old, she fought for freedom and for a better life, but now she was still poor, still without basic things. She said, "What does it mean when I am still living under the same conditions I was in then [under apartheid]?" As a matter of a fact, she said she wished that [she] had hanged and been spared the continued suffering. . . . I think it eats at people that many of the [perpetrators], even the people who went to the TRC and who testified and admitted what they had done, have gone back to their communities. They go to their churches; they continue to have their style of life; they are accepted in their communities. And the victims, like this woman, continue to live in poverty.

Joanna Nkosi
Historian, Consultant
Johannesburg, January 2007

You can live here as if nothing happened. You could swear you were in New York or in Paris the way people live, and yet there is a whole other world here where people are living in abject poverty. There's very glib speak in South Africa about,

"Let's talk and move on." But who says that? The beneficiaries of the transition and apartheid can move on, but the vast majority are left behind.

Yasmin Sooka
Former TRC Commissioner
Pretoria, March 2008

Criminal justice is only one part of a larger picture than includes both civil and social justice. A one-dimensional court-centered approach to transitional justice will be inherently limited, and is not the only effective mechanism for a public eager to gain a richer, clearer understanding of the past or to accomplish meaningful social transformation.

Trials are at best an imperfect tool if society's goal is not simply conviction of wrongdoers, but also to provide solace to victims, allowing them to gain public acknowledgement of the harms suffered and a truthful and complete account of past abuses. Procedural guarantees attendant to trials— for example, that evidence be admissible or relevant, in a strictly legal sense— protect the rights of the defendant, often at the expense of truth-seeking. The adversarial process is not always designed to unearth full historical accounts of the past, or to tie together distinct narratives to tell a coherent story, and is thus not ideally suited to broader goals related to reconciliation. Rather, trials focus on examination of witnesses, reviewing evidence about the responsibility of specific individuals, and determining guilt. Victims and witnesses must testify and endure cross-examination in a manner than often prevents them from directly and comprehensively narrating their experiences. The opportunity to tell one's story, uninterrupted and in a supportive rather than skeptical environment, is crucial to many survivors of human rights abuses but may not be realized in court, where a witness must testify to what she saw and heard rather than what she felt. The opportunity for individuals to heal and empower themselves by telling their story, and by learning the truth, are not the primary objectives of the justice system when pursuing prosecutions.

Accordingly, criminal prosecutions, alone, are too narrow to address persistent injustices. In South Africa, millions of citizens continue to reside in poverty and struggle to make ends meet, with limited access to basic social services and little promise of upward mobility. However, prosecutions need not simply be about convictions and imprisonment, but might also be used to advance more expansive notions of justice and reconciliation, thereby carrying forward the TRC's mission. The Constitutional Court recognized this imperative to seek broader justice in the *Azapo* judgment:

The families of those whose fundamental human rights were invaded by torture and abuse are not the only victims who have endured "untold suffering and injustice" in consequence of the crass inhumanity of apartheid which so many have had to endure for so long. Generations of children born and yet to be born will suffer the consequences of poverty, malnutrition, of homelessness, of illiteracy and disempowerment generated and sustained by the institutions of apartheid and its manifest effects on life and living for so many. . . . The resources of the state have to be deployed imaginatively, wisely, efficiently and equitably, to facilitate the reconstruction process in a manner which best brings relief and hope to the widest sections of the community, developing for the benefit of the entire nation the latent human potential and resources of every person who has directly or indirectly been burdened with the heritage of the shame and the pain of our racist past.[266]

South Africa has yet to adequately address the many indirect victims who suffered under apartheid, partially because the TRC's mandate to focus on gross human rights abuses rendered it unable to confront the broader indignities of apartheid or to examine the culpability of the nation as a whole.[267] As Yasmin Sooka explains:

One of the terrible effects of the Truth Commission was the kind of shifting of focus to trigger-pullers and the obsession of white South Africans that having had the Truth Commission, they can move on and nobody needs to deal with what apartheid was really about. That mistake must be fairly placed at our [the TRC's] feet. You do wonder if people were caught up in the euphoria of this new political order, so we didn't ask some of the right questions, those dealing with benefits and structure. We didn't demonstrate enough that any system [of oppression] needs support. Any system needs

---

[266] *Azanian People's Organization (AZAPO) and Others v. The President of the Republic of South Africa and Others*, 1996 (4) SA 671 (Const. Ct.), para. 43.

[267] Mahmood Mamdani, "Amnesty or Impunity? A Preliminary Critique of the Report of the Truth and Reconciliation of South Africa," *Diacritics*, Volume 32, No. 3/4 (Fall 2002), pp. 33-60.

the willing acquiescence and complicity of people who enjoy benefit. Apartheid was structural in the way in which it played itself out. If you look at where we are, what are we struggling with? We are struggling with this legacy, the structural legacy of apartheid. There is no acknowledgment by white people in my country that they benefited. I grapple with how you build a nation when you don't have a shared understanding of history. . . . If you listen to the way white people talk about this government, there is no acknowledgment that this whole framework we have is really the product of people wanting to reclaim their humanity, their dignity. That's what the whole constitutional process was about. . . . You have young people who say, "I wasn't there at the time." And I say, my dear, actually the legacy is a generational benefit. We have not yet talked about that.[268]

At its core, apartheid was an institutionalized system of repression and dispossession intended to enforce powerlessness among classes of people. Its legacy is social deprivation and inequality. The TRC did not create an environment where ordinary people who benefited from apartheid and were complicit in its abuses were forced to reflect on their role or made to actively contribute to the process of national rebuilding and reconciliation. As a result, apartheid's twin legacies of poverty and marginalization remain largely unaddressed, and social transformation has not been realized.

Prosecutions and restorative justice need not be mutually exclusive, however. Rather than being used as an avenue to divert attention away from other social justice issues, prosecutions might serve as an impetus and backdrop for social transformation. A renewed prosecutions strategy could spark discussions about the role of ordinary individuals in the crimes of the past, and might lead people to consider how they can acknowledge their culpability, make amends, and create programs and strategies to remedy persistent inequalities and restore the dignity of all South Africans. If creatively structured and implemented, prosecutions could focus attention not only on individual victims and perpetrators but also on broader issues of social justice like land redistribution, racism, education, economic empowerment, housing, and health care, which in turn could foster further reconciliation. Victims

---

[268] International Human Rights Clinic interview with Yasmin Sooka, Former TRC Commissioner, Attorney, Executive Director of the Foundation for Human Rights, Pretoria, South Africa, Mar. 26, 2008.

would be served, and perpetrators (those who are prosecuted) would be held to account for their past crimes and indiscretions.

V. CONCLUSION

The question of how to address apartheid-era crimes will likely remain a source of contestation in South Africa for years to come, and other transitional societies will undoubtedly confront similar, and equally vexing, challenges. Prosecutions are a crucial component of a transitional process, but they are neither a panacea nor the inevitable response to every human rights abuse; rather, they are one element of any continuing effort to achieve justice and reconciliation, and are most powerful when coupled with other mechanisms geared at broader social transformation. Equally important, transitional justice itself does not suddenly reach a clear conclusion, in South Africa or elsewhere. It is an ongoing process, made more effective when political leaders, civil society, and ordinary citizens participate together in seeking and achieving justice.

The TRC demonstrated both South Africa's willingness to confront the past in a thoughtful and sustained manner, as well as the ability of individuals to transcend adversity and emerge with dignity and strength. In carrying forward the transitional process and continuing to seek justice through prosecutions, reparations, or other mechanisms, South Africa would continue to transform itself as a nation.

Rather than feeling frustrated or hopeless, many South Africans persist in seeking ways to rebuild their society, consolidate democracy, and foster reconciliation. Legal frameworks and mechanisms can make a positive difference in how individuals and societies emerge from devastating atrocities. The history of post-apartheid South Africa is still being written but, as the closing Reflection vividly demonstrates, there is reason for hope.

REFLECTION

"Justice is an ongoing paradigm."

Jody Kollapen, Chairperson, South African Human Rights Commission
Johannesburg, October 2006

Going into the Truth and Reconciliation [Commission] process, we had a clear idea that there would be a changeover. [As members of civil society,] we thought that those responsible for human rights abuses would be held accountable because that was the norm. But the ANC negotiations with the old regime put amnesty on the table. We begrudgingly accepted amnesty even though it was not the traditional concept of justice. Civil society still wanted some form of accountability. But we lost.

Amnesty got stuck from the beginning. There was not a flood of applications to the TRC because people were nervous. A political intervention was necessary to say it was okay to come forward because people could qualify for amnesty. A good example is the first individual who was granted amnesty, Captain Brian Mitchell, who led an attack in KwaZulu-Natal on night vigil mourners.[269] There was the big question of proportionality: a grant of amnesty was not going to satisfy proportionality [criteria] in any way. But he was granted amnesty. It set a precedent and signaled to others that they could come forward. Amnesty did not unfold in terms of the [TRC] guidelines. There was a radical departure from the guidelines to create a climate where people would come forward.

The question of prosecutions was not a real issue for years. Prosecutors and perpetrators adopted a wait and see attitude to see if a process would unfold with amnesty and reparations to achieve justice. Ordinary victims said, "What's happening?" People were granted amnesty, and then they lived on with their pensions. The question of justice remained unanswered and unresolved. It is a factor in why we still need prosecutions: for reparations. There was not enough monetary compensation.

There were several issues that the TRC left unresolved. The TRC did not examine culpability of the nation as a whole. The focus was on the security system cog, but culpability on a national scale was the missing piece

---

[269] In December 1988, Mitchell and his special constables killed eleven people, mainly women and children, at a night vigil in Trust Feed. Mitchell's 30-year prison sentence for the eleven murders was expunged after he testified before the TRC's Amnesty Committee in 1996.

of the puzzle. There was an organization set up by a group of well meaning white South Africans called Home for All. It asked those who benefited from apartheid to set up a fund to build houses. It never really got off the ground, sadly, because the TRC process didn't create a space for ordinary South Africans to understand their contribution [to the apartheid system].

The TRC could have created an environment where ordinary people who benefited from apartheid, who weren't active but were complicit, would have been more willing to contribute to national rebuilding. The discussion of the role of ordinary South Africans doesn't happen because it's pegged on discussions of blame. The TRC made it seem like we'd identified the bad guys, so for white South Africans there was a distancing and after it was done they'd say, "Let's get on with our lives." What about sharing the resources in a more equitable way, or some acknowledgement of, "This is where I am, and this is where you are as a result of apartheid. What can I do to make right by you?"

Furthermore, to some extent the TRC prevented substantive discussion of civil liability. The process now with the current guidelines [on prosecutions] opens the door for that. There is room for reparations as part of the discussion, to say, "Look, if these are the consequences of my acts, this is what I'm willing to do." That's a price victims are willing to pay. For many victims they'd gladly take that rather than putting the perpetrator in jail, end of story. It is also closer to *ubuntu*, a justice that is restorative rather than retributive.

Now there is an undue focus on prosecutions as the only form of accountability for the past. Many people believe we need to merge [to] a new paradigm of justice. Criminal justice is only one part. There is still civil and broader social justice. The current debate about prosecutions takes away focus on other ends. It is an important issue, but it is problematic. Those most likely to be prosecuted are foot soldiers. [Prosecutors] are never going to get near the big fish. The evidence burden is substantial. In that sense, the targeting is done disproportionately; they're not near [prosecuting] those responsible for the plans and orders.

Frankly, many victims are not concerned with prosecutions, but only what happens in their lives. What concern[ed] me about the [constitutional] challenge is what it [did] for white South Africans: it acts as an avenue for diverting attention from other social justice issues. The focus is on a few victims and a few perpetrators. It is a nice diversion for not having to deal with land distribution, racism, transforming the justice system and economy, developing housing. Those issues should rank equally high in the transformation. [The constitutional challenge] pushes prosecutions to the forefront over other avenues [to justice] because it's an emotional debate. What's the difference between someone who is tortured and an entire community whose homes were destroyed and forced to move? In my view, it is hard to distinguish. The discussion of prosecutions should not be at the expense of other approaches to justice.

The guidelines don't preclude process. The TRC precluded civil litigation. The TRC could have ordered perpetrators to make good. If I were Desmond Tutu, I would have asked them to tack on something more substantive to their apologies. The NPA guidelines don't preclude something like that. Instead, they may encourage victims to come forward if they could get more than [imprisonment of perpetrators]—something that could change their lives in a material way.

There was a guy, I can't remember his name, who applied for and was granted amnesty for torturing an activist. The guy was doing well, running a security business. He approached the victim and said, "I'm doing okay. This isn't an act of charity. Why don't you join me as a partner?" And they are still in business. During this time, they've been able to talk about the past. For the victim, he was able to see change, real change, in his life. It was not charity but a business opportunity. That's a wonderful story about how a human wrong became a human right.

We must engage with the victims. I don't think there's been enough engagement with victims by civil society. The [constitutional] challenge is based on principles but is made without really understanding what victims' needs are. You can argue that current policies are meant to address this missing element through affirmative justice. But in truth and reality, they don't do that. I'm not sure with what integrity you can say to victims, "It is enough that we build one million houses in ten years." We need more discussion on how to address inequalities in our society with the recognition that that they came from our history. There is a group of retired white South Africans who have skills and approached the president to ask if their skills could be put to use by the country, to do trainings and so on. They would do so free of charge. These things are quite powerful. They don't address individual victims but focus on changing the environment. [In this way,] justice is an ongoing paradigm.

APPENDIX A

**Prosecuting Policy and Directives Relating to
the Prosecution of Offences Emanating from
Conflicts of the Past and Which Were Committed
on or Before 11 May 1994**

A. INTRODUCTION

1. In his statement to the National Houses of Parliament and the Nation, on 15 April 2003, President Thabo Mbeki, among others, gave Government's response to the Final Report of the Truth and Reconciliation Commission (TRC). The essential features of the response for the purpose of this new policy, are the following:

   (a) It was recognized that not all persons who qualified for amnesty availed themselves of the TRC process, for a variety of reasons, ranging from incorrect advice (legally or politically) or undue influence to a deliberate rejection of the process.

   (b) A continuation of the amnesty process of the TRC cannot be considered as this would constitute an infringement of the Constitution, especially as it would amount to a suspension of victims' rights and would fly in the face of the objectives of the TRC process. The question as to the prosecution or not of persons, who did not take part in the TRC process, is left in the hands of the National Prosecuting Authority (NPA) as is normal practice.

   (c) As part of the normal legal processes and in the national interest, the NPA, working with the Intelligence Agencies, will be accessible to those persons who are prepared to unearthing the truth of the conflicts of the past and who wish to enter into agreements that are standard in the normal execution of justice and the prosecuting mandate, and are accommodated in our legislation. Therefore, persons who had committed crimes, before 11 May 1994, which emanate from conflicts of the past, could enter into agreements with the prosecuting authority in accordance with existing legislation. This was stated in the context of the recognition of the need to gain a full understanding of the networks which operated at the relevant time since, in certain instances, these networks still operated and posed a threat to current security. Particular reference was made to un-recovered arms caches.

2. In view of the above, prosecuting policy, directives and guidelines are required to reflect and attach due weight to the following:

(a) The Human Rights culture which underscores the Constitution and the status accorded to victims in terms of the TRC and other legislation.
(b) The constitutional right to life.
(c) The non-prescriptivity of the crime of murder.
(d) The recognition that the process of transformation to democracy recognized the need to create a mechanism where persons who had committed politically motivated crimes, linked to the conflicts of the past, could receive indemnity or amnesty from prosecution.
(e) The *dicta* of the Constitutional Court justifying the constitutionality of the above process, *inter alia*, on the basis that it did not absolutely deprive victims of the right to prosecution in cases where amnesty had been refused. (See *Azanian Peoples Organisation v The President of the RSA, 1996 (8)BCLR 1015 CC*).
(f) The recommendation by the TRC that the NPA should consider prosecutions for persons who failed to apply for amnesty or who were refused amnesty.
(g) Government's response to the Final Report of the TRC as set out in paragraphs 1(a) to (d) above.
(h) The *dicta* of the Constitutional Court to the effect that the NPA represents the community and is under an international obligation to prosecute crimes of apartheid. (See *The State v Wouter Basson CCT 30/03.*)
(i) The constitutional obligation on the NPA to exercise its functions without fear, favour or prejudice (section 179 of the Constitution).
(j) The legal obligations placed on the NPA in terms of its enabling legislation, in particular the provisions relating to the formulation of prosecuting criteria and the right of persons affected by decisions of

the NPA to make representations, and for them to be dealt with.

(k) The existing prosecuting policy and general directives or guidelines issued by the National Director of Public Prosecutions (NDPP) to assist prosecutors in arriving at a decision to prosecute or not.

(l) The terms and conditions under which the Amnesty Committee of the TRC could consider applications for amnesty and the criteria for granting of amnesty for gross violation of human rights.

3. Government did not intend to mandate the NDPP to, under the auspice of his or her own office, perpetuate the TRC amnesty process. The existing legislation and normal process referred to by the President, include the following:

(a) Section 204 of the Criminal Procedure Act, 1977 (Act No. 51 of 1977), which provides that a person who is guilty of criminal conduct may testify on behalf of the State against his or her co-conspirators and if the Court trying the matter finds that he or she testified in a satisfactory manner, grant him or her indemnity from prosecution.

(b) Section 105A of the Criminal Procedure Act, 1977, which makes provision for a person who has committed a criminal offence to enter into a mutually acceptable guilty plea and sentence agreement with the NPA.

(c) Section 179(5) of the Constitution in terms of which the NDPP, among others—

  (i)   must determine, in consultation with the Minister and after consultation with the Directors of Public Prosecutions, prosecution policy to be observed in the prosecution process;

  (ii) must issue policy directives to be observed in the prosecution process; and

  (iii) may review a decision to prosecute or not to prosecute.

(d) The above process would not indemnify such a person from private prosecution or civil liability.

4. The NPA has a general discretion not to prosecute in cases where a *prima facie* case has been established and where it is of the view that such a prosecution would not be in the public interest. The factors to be considered include the following:

(a) The fact that the victim does not desire prosecution.
(b) The severity of the crime in question.
(c) The strength of the case.
(d) The cost of the prosecution weighed against the sentence likely to be imposed.
(e) The interests of the community and the public interest.

In the event of the NPA declining to prosecute in such an instance, such a person is not protected against a private prosecution.

5. Therefore, following Government's response, and the equality provisions in our Constitution and the equality legislation, and taking into account the above factors regarding the handling of cases arising from conflicts of the past, which were committed prior to 11 May 1994, it is important to deal with these matters on a rational, uniform, effective and reconciliatory basis in terms of specifically defined prosecutorial policies, directives and guidelines.

B. PROCEDURAL ARRANGEMENTS WHICH MUST BE ADHERED TO IN THE PROSECUTION PROCESS IN RESPECT OF CRIMES ARISING FROM CONFLICTS OF THE PAST

The following procedure must be strictly adhered to in respect of persons wanting to make representations to the NDPP, and in respect of those cases already received by the Office of the NDPP, relating to alleged offences arising from conflicts of the past and which were committed before 11 May 1994:

1. A person who faces possible prosecution and who wishes to enter into arrangements with the NPA, as contemplated in paragraph A1 above (the Applicant), must submit a written sworn affidavit or solemn affirmation to the NDPP containing such representations.
2. The NDPP must confirm receipt of the affidavit or affirmation and may request further particulars by way of a written sworn affidavit or solemn affirmation from the Applicant. The Applicant may also *mero moto* submit a further written sworn affidavit or solemn affirmation to the NDPP containing representations.
3. All such representations must contain a full disclosure of all the facts, factors or circumstances surrounding the commission of the alleged offence, including all information which may uncover any network,

person or thing, which posed a threat to our security at any stage or may pose a threat to our current security.

4. The Priority Crimes Litigation Unit (PCLU) in the Office of the NDPP shall be responsible for overseeing investigations and instituting prosecutions in all such matters.

5. The regional Directors of Public Prosecutions must refer all prosecutions arising from the conflicts of the past, which were committed before 11 May 1994, and with which they are or may be seized, immediately to the Office of the NDPP.

6. The PCLU shall be assisted in the execution of its duties by a senior designated official from the following State departments or other components of the NPA:

(a) The National Intelligence Agency.
(b) The Detective Division of the South African Police Service.
(c) The Department of Justice & Constitutional Development.
(d) The Directorate of Special Operations.

7. The NDPP must approve all decisions to continue an investigation or prosecution or not, or to prosecute or not to prosecute.

8. The NDPP must also be consulted in respect of and approve any offer to a perpetrator relating to the bestowing of the status of a section 204 witness and all section 105A plea and sentence agreements.

9. The NDPP may obtain the views of any private or public person or institution, our intelligence agencies and the Commissioner of the South African Police Service, and must obtain the views of any victims, as far as is reasonably possible, before arriving at a decision.

10. A decision of the NDPP not to prosecute and the reasons for that decision must be made public.

11. In accordance with section 179 (6) of the Constitution, the NDPP must inform the Minister for Justice & Constitutional Development of all decisions taken or intended to be taken in respect of this prosecuting policy relating to conflicts of the past.

12. The NDPP may make public statements on any matter arising from this policy relating to conflicts of the past, where such statements are necessary in the interests of good governance and transparency, but only after informing the Minister for Justice and Constitutional Development thereof.

13. The institution of any prosecution in terms of this policy relating

to conflicts of the past would not deprive the accused from making further representations to the NDPP requesting the NDPP to withdraw the charges against him or her. These representations would be considered according to the NPA prosecuting policy, directives, guidelines and established practice. The victims must, as far as reasonably possible, be consulted in any such further process and be informed, should the accused's representations be successful.

14. The NDPP may provide for any additional procedures.
15. All state agencies, in particular those dealing with the prosecution of alleged offenders and those responsible for the investigation of offences, must be requested not to use any information obtained from an alleged accused person during this process in any subsequent criminal trial against such a person. Whatever the response of such agencies may be to this request, the NPA records that its policy in this regard is not to make use of such information at any stage of the prosecuting process, especially not to present it in evidence in any subsequent criminal trial against such person.

C. CRITERIA GOVERNING THE DECISION TO PROSECUTE OR NOT TO PROSECUTE IN CASES RELATING TO CONFLICTS OF THE PAST

Apart from the general criteria set out in paragraph 4 of the Prosecuting Policy of the NPA, the following criteria are determined for the prosecution of cases arising from conflicts of the past:

1. The alleged offence must have been committed on or before 11 May 1994.
2. Whether a prosecution can be instituted on the strength of adequate evidence after applying the general criteria set out in paragraph 4 of the said Prosecuting Policy of the NPA.
3. If the answers to paragraphs 1 and 2 above are in the affirmative, then the further criteria in paragraphs (a) to (j) hereunder, must, in a balanced way, be applied by the NDPP before reaching a decision whether to prosecute or not:

(a) Whether the alleged offender has made a full disclosure of all relevant facts, factors or circumstances to the alleged act, omission or offence.
(b) Whether the alleged act, omission or offence is an act associated with

a political objective committed in the course of conflicts of the past. In reaching a decision in this regard the following factors must be considered:

(i) The motive of the person who committed the act, commission or offence.

(ii) The object or objective of the act, omission or offence, and in particular whether the act, omission or offence was primarily directed at a political opponent or State property or personnel or against private property or individuals.

(iii) Whether the act, omission or offence was committed in the execution of an order of, or on behalf of, or with the approval of, the organisation, institution, liberation movement or body of which the person who committed the act was a member, agent or a supporter.

(iv) The relationship between the act, omission or offence and the political objective pursued, and in particular the directness and proximity of the relationship and the proportionality of the act, omission or offence to the objective pursued, but does not include any act, omission or offence committed—

    (aa)   for personal gain; or

    (bb)   out of personal malice, ill-will or spite, directed against the victim of the act or offence committed.

(c) The degree of co-operation on the part of the alleged offender, including the alleged offenders endeavours to expose—

    (i)   the truth of the conflicts of the past, including the location of the remains of victims; or

    (ii)   possible clandestine operations during the past years of conflict, including exposure of networks that operated or are operating against the people, especially if such networks still pose a real or latent danger against our democracy.

(d) The personal circumstances of the alleged offender, in particular—

    (i)   whether the ill-health of or other humanitarian consideration relating to the alleged offender may justify the non-prosecution of the case;

    (ii)   the credibility of the alleged offender;

    (iii)   the alleged offender's sensitivity to the need for restitution;

    (iv)   the degree of remorse shown by the alleged offender and his or her attitude towards reconciliation;

    (v)   renunciation of violence and willingness to abide by the Constitution on the part of the alleged offender; and

      (vi)   the degree of indoctrination to which the alleged offender was subjected.

(e) Whether the offence in question is serious.

(f) The extent to which the prosecution or non-prosecution of the alleged offender may contribute, facilitate or undermine our national project of nation-building through transformation, reconciliation, development and reconstruction within and of our society.

(g) Whether the prosecution may lead to the further or renewed traumatisation of victims and conflicts in areas where reconciliation has already taken place.

(h) If relevant, the alleged offender's role during the TRC process, namely, in respect of co-operation, full disclosure and assisting the process in general.

(i) Consideration of any views obtained for purposes of reaching a decision.

(j) Any further criteria, which might be deemed necessary by the prosecutingauthority for reaching a decision.

APPENDIX B

Promotion of National Unity and Reconciliation Act
(Act No. 34 of 1995, The "TRC ACT")

To provide for the investigation and the establishment of as complete a picture as possible of the nature, causes and extent of gross violations of human rights committed during the period from 1 March 1960 to the cut-off date contemplated in the Constitution [6 December 1993], within or outside the Republic, emanating from the conflicts of the past, and the fate or whereabouts of the victims of such violations; the granting of amnesty to persons who make full disclosure of all the relevant facts relating to acts associated with a political objective committed in the course of the conflicts of the past during the said period; affording victims an opportunity to relate the violations they suffered; the taking of measures aimed at the granting of reparation to, and the rehabilitation and the restoration of the human and civil dignity of, victims of violations of human rights; reporting to the Nation about such violations and victims; the making of recommendations aimed at the prevention of the commission of gross violations of human rights; and for the said purposes to provide for the establishment of a Truth and Reconciliation Commission, a Committee on Human Rights Violations, a Committee on Amnesty and a Committee on Reparation and Rehabilitation; and to confer certain powers on, assign certain functions to and impose certain duties upon that Commission and those Committees; and to provide for matters connected therewith.

SINCE the Constitution of the Republic of South Africa, 1993 (Act No. 200 of 1993), provides a historic bridge between the past of a deeply divided society characterized by strife, conflict, untold suffering and injustice, and a future founded on the recognition of human rights, democracy and peaceful co-existence for all South Africans, irrespective of colour, race, class, belief or sex; AND SINCE it is deemed necessary to establish the truth in relation to past events as well as the motives for and circumstances in which gross violations of human fights have occurred, and to make the findings known in order to prevent a repetition of such acts in future; AND SINCE the Constitution states that the pursuit of national unity, the well-being of all South African citizens and peace require reconciliation between the people of South Africa and the reconstruction of society; AND SINCE the Constitution states that there is a need for understanding but not for vengeance, a need for reparation but not for retaliation, a need for ubuntu but not for victimization; AND SINCE the Constitution states that in order to advance such reconciliation and reconstruction amnesty shall be granted in respect of acts, omissions and offences associated with political objectives committed in the course of the conflicts of the past; AND SINCE the Constitution provides that Parliament shall under the Constitution adopt a law which determines a firm cut-off date, which shall be a date after 8 October 1990 and before the cut-off date envisaged in the Constitution, and providing for the mechanisms, criteria and procedures, including tribunals, if any, through which such amnesty shall be dealt with; . . .

Section 20

1. If the Committee, after considering an application for amnesty, is satisfied that—
(a) the application complies with the requirements of this Act;
(b) the act, omission or offence to which the application relates is an act associated with a political objective committed in the course of the conflicts of the past in accordance with the provisions of subsections (2) and (3); and
(c) the applicant has made a full disclosure of all relevant facts, it shall grant amnesty in respect of that act, omission or offence.

2. In this Act, unless the context otherwise indicates, "act associated with a political objective" means any act or omission which constitutes an offence or delict which, according to the criteria in subsection (3), is associated with a political objective, and which was advised, planned, directed, commanded, ordered or committed within or outside the Republic during the period I March 1960 to the cut-off date, by—
(a) any member or supporter of a publicly known political organisation or liberation movement on behalf of or in support of such organisation or movement, bona fide in furtherance of a political struggle waged by such organisation or movement against the State or any former state or another publicly known political organisation or liberation movement;
(b) any employee of the State or any former state or any member of

the security forces of the State or any former state in the course and scope of his or her duties and within the scope of his or her express or implied authority directed against a publicly known political organisation or liberation movement engaged in a political struggle against the State or a former state or against any members or supporters of such organisation or movement, and which was committed bona fide with the object of countering or otherwise resisting the said struggle;

(c) any employee of the State or any former state or any member of the security forces of the State or any former state in the course and scope of his or her duties and within the scope of his or her express or implied authority directed—

(i)   in the case of the State, against any former state; or

(ii)   in the case of a former state, against the State or any other former state, whilst engaged in a political struggle against each other or against any employee of the State or such former state, as the case may be, and which was committed bona fide with the object of countering or otherwise resisting the said struggle;

(d) any employee or member of a publicly known political organisation or liberation movement in the course and scope of his or her duties and within the scope of his or her express or implied authority directed against the State or any former state or any publicly known political organisation or liberation movement engaged in a political struggle against that political organisation or liberation movement or against members of the security forces of the State or any former state or members or supporters of such publicly known political organisation or liberation movement, and which was committed bona fide in furtherance of the said struggle;

(e) any person in the performance of a coup d'etat to take over the government of any former state, or in any attempt thereto;

(f) any person referred to in paragraphs (a), (b), (c) and (d), who on reasonable grounds believed that he or she was acting in the course and scope of his or her duties and within the scope of his or her express or implied authority;

(g) any person who associated himself or herself with any act or omission committed for the purposes referred to in paragraphs (a), (b), (c), (d), (e) and (f).

3. Whether a particular act, omission or offence contemplated in
    subsection (2) is an act associated with a political objective, shall be
    decided with reference to the following criteria:

(a) the motive of the person who committed the act, omission or offence;

(b) the context in which the act, omission or offence took place, and in
    particular whether the act, omission or offence was committed in the
    course of or as part of a political uprising, disturbance or event, or in
    reaction thereto;

(c) the legal and factual nature of the act, omission or offence, including
    the gravity of the act, omission or offence;

(d) the object or objective of the act, omission or offence, and in particular
    whether the act, omission or offence was primarily directed at a
    political opponent or State property or personnel or against private
    property or individuals;

(e) whether the act, omission or offence was committed in the execution
    of an order of, or on behalf of, or with the approval of, the organisation,
    institution, liberation movement or body of which the person who
    committed the act was a member, an agent or a supporter; and

(f) the relationship between the act, omission or offence and the political
    objective pursued, and in particular the directness and proximity of
    the relationship and the proportionality of the act, omission or offence
    to the objective pursued, but does not include any act, omission or
    offence committed by any person referred to in subsection (2) who
    acted-

    (i)   for personal gain: Provided that an act, omission or offence
          by any person who acted and received money or anything of
          value as an informer of the State or a former state, political
          organisation or liberation movement, shall not be excluded
          only on the grounds of that person having received money or
          anything of value for his or her information;

    (ii) out of personal malice, ill-will or spite, directed against the
          victim of the acts committed.

4. In applying the criteria contemplated in subsection (3), the Committee
    shall take into account the criteria applied in the Acts repealed by
    section 48.

5. The Commission shall inform the person concerned and, if possible,

any victim, of the decision of the Committee to grant amnesty to such person in respect of a specified act, omission or offence and the Committee shall submit to the Commission a record of the proceedings, which may, subject to the provisions of this Act, be used by the Commission.

APPENDIX C

CRIMINAL PROCEDURE ACT
(ACT NO. 51 OF 1977)

105A. Plea and sentence agreements.

(1) *(a)* A prosecutor authorised thereto in writing by the National Director of Public Prosecutions and an accused who is legally represented may, before the accused pleads to the charge brought against him or her, negotiate and enter into an agreement in respect of—

    (i) a plea of guilty by the accused to the offence charged or to an offence of which he or she may be convicted on the charge; and

    (ii) if the accused is convicted of the offence to which he or she has agreed to plead guilty—

        (a) a just sentence to be imposed by the court; or

        (b) the postponement of the passing of sentence in terms of section 297 (1) (*a*); or

        (c) a just sentence to be imposed by the court, of which the operation of the whole or any part thereof is to be suspended in terms of section 297 (1) (*b*); and

        (d) if applicable, an award for compensation as contemplated in section 300.

  (b) The prosecutor may enter into an agreement contemplated in paragraph (*a*)—

    (i) after consultation with the person charged with the investigation of the case;

    (ii) with due regard to, at least, the—

        (a) nature of and circumstances relating to the offence;

        (b) personal circumstances of the accused;

        (c) previous convictions of the accused, if any; and

        (d) interests of the community, and

    (iii) after affording the complainant or his or her representative, where it is reasonable to do so and taking into account the nature of and circumstances relating to the offence and

the interests of the complainant, the opportunity to make
representations to the prosecutor regarding—
  (a) the contents of the agreement; and
  (b) the inclusion in the agreement of a condition relating
       to compensation or the rendering to the complainant of
       some specific benefit or service in lieu of compensation for
       damage or pecuniary loss.
  (c) The requirements of paragraph *(b)* (i) may be dispensed with if the
       prosecutor is satisfied that consultation with the person charged with
       the investigation of the case will delay the proceedings to such an
       extent that it could—
    (i)   cause substantial prejudice to the prosecution, the accused, the
          complainant or his or her representative; and
    (ii) affect the administration of justice adversely.
(2) An agreement contemplated in subsection (1) shall be in writing and shall
    at least—
  (a) state that the accused, before entering into the agreement, has been
       informed that he or she has the right—
    (i)   to be presumed innocent until proved guilty beyond reasonable
          doubt;
    (ii) to remain silent and not to testify during the proceedings; and
    (iii) not to be compelled to give self-incriminating evidence;
  (b) state fully the terms of the agreement, the substantial facts of the
       matter, all other facts relevant to the sentence agreement and any
       admissions made by the accused;
  (c) be signed by the prosecutor, the accused and his or her legal
       representative; and
  (d) if the accused has negotiated with the prosecutor through an
       interpreter, contain a certificate by the interpreter to the effect that he
       or she interpreted accurately during the negotiations and in respect of
       the contents of the agreement.
(3) The court shall not participate in the negotiations contemplated in
    subsection (1).
(4) *(a)* The prosecutor shall, before the accused is required to plead, inform the
    court that an agreement contemplated in subsection (1) has been entered
    into and the court shall then—
    (i)   require the accused to confirm that such an agreement has been
          entered into; and
    (ii) satisfy itself that the requirements of subsection (1) *(b)* (i) and

(iii) have been complied with.

(b) If the court is not satisfied that the agreement complies with the requirements of subsection (1) (b) (i) and (iii), the court shall—

    (i) inform the prosecutor and the accused of the reasons for noncompliance; and

    (ii) afford the prosecutor and the accused the opportunity to comply with the requirements concerned.

(5) If the court is satisfied that the agreement complies with the requirements of subsection (1) (b) (i) and (iii), the court shall require the accused to plead to the charge and order that the contents of the agreement be disclosed in court.

(6) (a) After the contents of the agreement have been disclosed, the court shall question the accused to ascertain whether—

    (i) he or she confirms the terms of the agreement and the admissions made by him or her in the agreement;

    (ii) with reference to the alleged facts of the case, he or she admits the allegations in the charge to which he or she has agreed to plead guilty; and

    (iii) the agreement was entered into freely and voluntarily in his or her sound and sober senses and without having been unduly influenced.

(b) After an inquiry has been conducted in terms of paragraph (a), the court shall, if—

    (i) the court is not satisfied that the accused is guilty of the offence in respect of which the agreement was entered into; or

    (ii) it appears to the court that the accused does not admit an allegation in the charge or that the accused has incorrectly admitted any such allegation or that the accused has a valid defence to the charge; or

    (iii) for any other reason, the court is of the opinion that the plea of guilty by the accused should not stand, record a plea of not guilty and inform the prosecutor and the accused of the reasons therefor.

(c) If the court has recorded a plea of not guilty, the trial shall start *de novo* before another presiding officer: Provided that the accused may waive his or her right to be tried before another presiding officer.

(7) (a) If the court is satisfied that the accused admits the allegations in the charge and that he or she is guilty of the offence in respect of which the agreement was entered into, the court shall proceed to consider the

sentence agreement.

    (b) For purposes of paragraph *(a)*, the court—

        (ii) may—

            (a) direct relevant questions, including questions about the previous convictions of the accused, to the prosecutor and the accused; and

            (b) hear evidence, including evidence or a statement by or on behalf of the accused or the complainant; and

        (iii) must, if the offence concerned is an offence—

            (a) referred to in the Schedule to the Criminal Law Amendment Act, 1997 (Act No. 105 of 1997); or

            (b) for which a minimum penalty is prescribed in the law creating the offence, have due regard to the provisions of that Act or law.

(8) If the court is satisfied that the sentence agreement is just, the court shall inform the prosecutor and the accused that the court is so satisfied, whereupon the court shall convict the accused of the offence charged and sentence the accused in accordance with the sentence agreement.

(9) *(a)* If the court is of the opinion that the sentence agreement is unjust, the court shall inform the prosecutor and the accused of the sentence which it considers just.

    (b) Upon being informed of the sentence which the court considers just, the prosecutor and the accused may—

        (i) abide by the agreement with reference to the charge and inform the court that, subject to the right to lead evidence and to present argument relevant to sentencing, the court may proceed with the imposition of sentence; or

        (ii) withdraw from the agreement

    (c) If the prosecutor and the accused abide by the agreement as contemplated in paragraph *(b)* (i), the court shall convict the accused of the offence charged and impose the sentence which it considers just.

    (d) If the prosecutor or the accused withdraws from the agreement as contemplated in paragraph *(b)* (ii), the trial shall start *de novo* before another presiding officer: Provided that the accused may waive his or her right to be tried before another presiding officer.

(10) Where a trial starts *de novo* as contemplated in subsection (6) *(c)* or (9) *(d)*—

    (a) the agreement shall be null and void and no regard shall be had or reference made to—

(i) any negotiations which preceded the entering into the agreement;

(ii) the agreement; or

(iii) any record of the agreement in any proceedings relating thereto, unless the accused consents to the recording of all or certain admissions made by him or her in the agreement or during any proceedings relating thereto and any admission so recorded shall stand as proof of such admission;

(b) the prosecutor and the accused may not enter into a plea and sentence agreement in respect of a charge arising out of the same facts; and

(c) the prosecutor may proceed on any charge.

(11)(a) The National Director of Public Prosecutions, in consultation with the Minister, shall issue directives regarding all matters which are reasonably necessary or expedient to be prescribed in order to achieve the objects of this section and any directive so issued shall be observed in the application of this section.

(b) The directives contemplated in paragraph (a)—

(i) must prescribe the procedures to be followed in the application of this section relating to—

(a) any offence referred to in the Schedule to the Criminal Law Amendment Act, 1997, or any other offence for which a minimum penalty is prescribed in the law creating the offence;

(b) any offence in respect of which a court has the power or is required to conduct a specific enquiry, whether before or after convicting or sentencing the accused; and

(c) any offence in respect of which a court has the power or is required to make a specific order upon conviction of the accused;

(ii) may prescribe the procedures to be followed in the application of this section relating to any other offence in respect of which the National Director of Public Prosecutions deems it necessary or expedient to prescribe specific procedures;

(iii) must ensure that adequate disciplinary steps shall be taken against a prosecutor who fails to comply with any directive; and

(iv) must ensure that comprehensive records and statistics relating to the implementation and application of this section are kept by the prosecuting authority.

(c) The National Director of Public Prosecutions shall submit directives issued under this subsection to Parliament before those directives take effect, and the first directives so issued, must be submitted to Parliament within four months of the commencement of this section.

   (d) Any directive issued under this subsection may be amended or withdrawn in like manner.

(12) The National Director of Public Prosecutions shall at least once every year submit the records and statistics referred to in subsection (11) *(b) (iv)* to Parliament

(13) In this section "sentence agreement" means an agreement contemplated in subsection (1) (a) (ii).

[S. 105A inserted by s. 2 of Act No. 62 of 2001.]

204. Incriminating evidence by witness for prosecution.

(1) Whenever the prosecutor at criminal proceedings informs the court that any person called as a witness on behalf of the prosecution will be required by the prosecution to answer questions which may incriminate such witness with regard to an offence specified by the prosecutor—

   (a) the court, if satisfied that such witness is otherwise a competent witness for the prosecution, shall inform such witness—

      (i)   that he is obliged to give evidence at the proceedings in question;

      (ii)   that questions may be put to him which may incriminate him with regard to the offence specified by the prosecutor;

      (iii)   that he will be obliged to answer any question put to him, whether by the prosecution, the accused or the court, notwithstanding that the answer may incriminate him with regard to the offence so specified or with regard to any offence in respect of which a verdict of guilty would be competent upon a charge relating to the offence so specified;

      (iv)   that if he answers frankly and honestly all questions put to him, he shall be discharged from prosecution with regard to the offence so specified and with regard to any offence in respect of which a verdict of guilty would be competent upon a charge relating to the offence so specified; and

   (b) such witness shall thereupon give evidence and answer any question put to him, whether by the prosecution, the accused or the court, notwithstanding that the reply thereto may incriminate him with regard to the offence so specified by the prosecutor or with regard to any offence in respect of which a verdict of guilty would be competent

upon a charge relating to the offence so specified.

(2) If a witness referred to in subsection (1), in the opinion of the court, answers frankly and honestly all questions put to him—

(a) such witness shall, subject to the provisions of subsection (3), be discharged from prosecution for the offence so specified by the prosecutor and for any offence in respect of which a verdict of guilty would be competent upon a charge relating to the offence so specified; and

(b) the court shall cause such discharge to be entered on the record of the proceedings in question.

(3) The discharge referred to in subsection (2) shall be of no legal force or effect if it is given at preparatory examination proceedings and the witness concerned does not at any trial arising out of such preparatory examination, answer, in the opinion of the court, frankly and honestly all questions put to him at such trial, whether by the prosecution, the accused or the court.

(4) (a) Where a witness gives evidence under this section and is not discharged from prosecution in respect of the offence in question, such evidence shall not be admissible in evidence against him at any trial in respect of such offence or any offence in respect of which a verdict of guilty is competent upon a charge relating to such offence.

(b) The provisions of this subsection shall not apply with reference to a witness who is prosecuted for perjury arising from the giving of the evidence in question, or for a contravention of section 319 (3) of the Criminal Procedure Act, 1955 (Act 56 of 1955).

[Para. (b) amended by s. 1 of Act No. 49 of 1996.]

APPENDIX D

IN THE HIGH COURT OF SOUTH AFRICA

(TRANSKEI DIVISION)

In the matter between: CASE NO.125/04

THE STATE
and
KHWEZI NGOMA
ACCUSED NO.1
LITHA NTHLABATHI   ACCUSED
NO.2
VUMILE NKITHI
ACCUSED NO.3
MANDLA PHALAPHALA
ACCUSED NO.4

PLEA AND SENTENCE AGREEMENT
IN TERMS OF SECTION 105 A OF ACT 51 OF 1977

THE PARTIES

1.   Khwezi Ngoma No.1 a 36 year old South African male residing at No.2 Ralph Street Alice.

2.   Litha Ntlabathi [sic] accused No.2 a 36 year old South African male residing at No. 2093 Cuba Township Butterworth.

3.   Vumile Nkithi accused No.3 a 35 year old South African male residing at No. 5629 Vuli Valley Butterworth.

4.   Mandla Phalaphala accused No.4 a 32 year old South African male
        residing at Maduna Street Dutywa.

5.   Nothemba Mlonzi of Mlonzi and Co. Incorporated, the legal
        representative at all the accused.

6.   The State, as represented by the National Prosecuting Authority in the
        person of Adv. MC Mhaga. ("the Prosecutor")

hereby enter into an agreement in respect of a plea of guilty in terms of section 105
A(1)(a)(i) of Act 51 of 1977 ("the Act") ("the Plea Agreement") and sentence in
terms of section 105 A(1)(a)(ii) of the Act ("the sentence") to secure a conviction
of the accused on the charges outlined in the indictment and the admissions
herein contained, and to be sentenced as provided for in this agreement.

AUTHORITY FROM THE NATIONAL DIRECTOR OF PUBLIC PROSECUTIONS AND LEGAL OBLIGATIONS OF THE PROSECUTOR

7.1   The Prosecutor is duly authorized in writing by the National Director of
        Public Prosecutions to enter into this agreement in terms of section 105
        A (1) (a) of the Act as appears from Annexure A hereto.

7.2   The Prosecutor has consulted with Captain A.B. Hanise who is charged
        with the investigation of this case. He supports this plea and sentence
        agreement.

7.3   The Prosecutor has also consulted with all the relevant victims in the
        matter and they support this plea and sentence agreement.

7.4   The Prosecutor has consulted with the National Director of Public
        Prosecutions, Adv. V. Pikoli, who has indicated that he supports this
        plea and sentence agreement.

7.5   The Prosecutor further confirms that he entered into this agreement with
        the necessary cognisance of the nature and circumstances relating to the
        offence, the personal circumstances of the accused and the interests of
        the community.

RECOGNITION BY THE ACCUSED OF THEIR RIGHTS

8.   The accused admit that before entering into this agreement they were informed that they have the right:

8.1   to be presumed innocent until proven guilty beyond a reasonable doubt;

1.2   to remain silent and not to testify during the proceedings; and

1.3   not to be compelled to give self-incriminating evidence.

THE TERMS OF THE PLEA AGREEMENT, SUBSTANTIAL FACTS AND ADMISSIONS MADE BY THE ACCUSED AS TO SUCH AGREEMENT

9.   The parties agree that the accused will tender a plea of guilty to offences listed in the indictment, Annexure C attached hereto.

10.   The accused admit that:

10.1   During 1994 accused No.1, 2 and 3 were students at Butterworth College of Education and accused No.4 was a pupil at Ngubethole Junior Secondary School.

10.2   They were organised under the banner of Pan Africanist Students Organisation and later recruited for the internal wing of Azanian Peoples [sic] Liberation Army (APLA) under the auspices of the Pan Africanist Congress.

10.3   They had been recruited as members of APLA which was operating a military camp in Butterworth as part of intensifying their armed struggle.

10.4   On the 28 March 1994 the accused, under the command of Siphiwo Xotyeni, who was their commander and has since died, armed themselves with R5 rifle, 38 Revolver, Z88 pistol and M26 hand grenade.

10.5   They proceeded to Willowvale police station during the night in order to get arms which were to be used in APLA operations.

10.6   On arrival at the said police station they found Sgt. Sobantu Tsipa
        ("deceased") and Sgt. Lulama Binase ("complainant in count 2") on duty
        at the charge office.

10.7   The accused demanded firearms from two policemen and when they
        resisted they fired shots at them resulting in death of Sgt. Tsipa and
        injuring Sgt Binase. They robbed a service pistol, to wit a Z88 9mm
        parabellum from Sgt. Binase.

10.8   The deceased died as a result of "severe internal bleeding from shots on
        abdomen".

10.9   Their actions were unlawful and find no justification in law.

10.10   At all material times before, during and after the commission of these
        offences, they acted in concert in furtherance of a common purpose.

11.   The parties therefore agree that the accused are guilty of all the offences
        listed in the indictment.

THE TERMS OF THE SENTENCE AGREEMENT SUBSTANTIAL FACTS AND ADMISSIONS MADE BY THE ACCUSED AS TO SUCH AGREEMENT (INCLUDING MITIGATING AND AGGRAVATING FACTORS)

12.   The parties agree that the substantial facts and admissions recorded in
        the plea Agreement ought to be incorporated insofar as the facts are
        relevant to the sentence Agreement.

12.1   **PRIMARILY IN MITIGATION OF SENTENCE THE FOLLOWING
        SUBMISSIONS ARE MADE AND AGREED TO.**

12.2   Background to the commission of the offence charged. The four accused
        1, 2 and 3 students at Butterworth College of Education and 4 a standard
        7 scholar at Ngubethole Junior Secondary School, were organized
        under the banner of the Pan Africanist Students Organisation and later
        recruited for the internal wing of the Azanian People's Liberation Army
        (APLA) under the auspices of the Pan Africanist Congress.

12.3   The three students and a scholar, now accused were commanded by

Siphiwo Xotyeni (now deceased) who was allegedly from exile. In line with their party discipline they had to take command without questioning.

12.4 Their strategy was to make selective forays against institutions of the regime in the process amass weaponry to let the apartheid regime succumb to Africanist majority rule; freedom [sic].

12.5 Leadership of the military wing was primarily based in exile. Those who claim to be coming from exile were leaders, heroes, commanders and political commissars; their message was a command, and their command law. They had sacrificed their lives to liberate the country and therefore Apla [sic] cadres had taken an oath termed "serve suffer sacrifice".

12.6 Young, immature, highly revolutionarized, they went through the pain and the agony that characterized the conflict among South Africans over the decades. They were sensitized to fight for freedom and had to obey the orders of those who were said to be in charge and claim to be from "outside" the country coming home with commands to liberate the country. They joined and took commands religiously with other patriots to whom freedom meant life itself.

They stand today alone, for what they stood for the nation.

12.7 The background and the facts of this case present some circumstances that are so exceptional in nature determined by the peculiar characteristics of the nation at the time, that so obviously express a compelling conclusion that the imposition of a term of imprisonment would be shocking injustice to the accused.

1.8 <u>AMNESTY</u>

Although there was a democratic process by way of Truth and Reconciliation Commission for the accused to apply for amnesty, they never did. This is due to the fact that they were misled by their leadership to treat the process with disdain and that they expected the political leadership of the State institutions to which they belonged to provide the overall context against which they could present their cases.

As a result thereof, the four accused, not of the making of their own, missed the opportunity to usurp a critical trade off between normal judicial process on the one hand and the establishment of the truth and amnesty on the other hand.

As it were accused missed the trade off opportunity, which in all probability they would have presented their case with impunity.

The accused humbly submit and plead with this Honourable court to take into consideration that they at all times fell into the category of those who were designated by the machinery of transformation as falling outside the caliber of prison inmates.

Personal circumstances
Mandla Phalaphala
Born 1971
Resident-Dutywa, Eastern Cape.
Married with 7 dependants (six children and one niece)
Self employed—bus owner—sole bread winner
Was 23 years at the time of the commission of the offence and doing standard 7.

Kwezi Khaya Ngoma [sic]
Resident in Alice
Born 02 April 1970
Married with 7 dependants including wife
Parents both deceased,
Obtained BCOM degree at the University of Fort Hare in 1992
Worked for Fort Hare University, 1996-1999 as a junior lecturer
Currently a Councilor at Nkonkobe Municipality.
He was 22 years old at the time of the commission of the offence studying at Fort Hare.

Vumile Nkinti [sic]
Born 01-01-1970
Married with 3 children, parents and two brothers depending on him.
Qualified as a teacher in 1995, Butterworth College of Education.
Currently at teacher at Mntuyedwa J.S.S

Participating in Agriculture Youth.

He was 22 years at the time of the commission of the offence, studying at Butterworth College of Education.

Litha Ntlabathi [sic]

Born: 01-03-1970

Resident 2093 Cuba Township, Butterworth

Qualified teacher: Butterworth College of Education in 1994.

BA Education: University of Transkei in 1998.

Advanced Certificate in Education: Eastern Cape Technikon 2006.

Community Participation:

Provincial Negotiation Adjudicator (debate): Love Life 2005 Local organizing Committee member, Love life Chairperson English Subject Association, Butterworth District Sports chairperson, Xilinxa Senior Secondary School.

Occupation:

Educator—Xilinxa Senior Secondary School member of School Management Team.

Dependants: Fiance, his son, a brother and a sister.

The parties agree that:

1.1   The accused have no previous convictions.

1.2   The accused were 22-23 years old at the time of the commission of the offence.

1.3   The accused have responsibilities and are contributing to economic activity, growth and advancement of the country.

1.4   The accused had no personal benefit to derive from the commission of the offence. It was not committed in pursuit of greed nor abject cruelty, but by utilization and political pursuit.

1.5   The parties agree that the provisions of Section 51 of Act 105 of 1997 are not applicable to the offence to which the accused are indicted and have pleaded guilty.

Aggravating Factors

1.1   The victims were both law enforcement officers who were on duty.

1.2   The deceased constitutionally entrenched right to life was grossly violated and importance of human life can never be over emphasized.

14.2   [sic] Although the attack was politically motivated many political parties had abandoned the armed struggle and country was approaching its first democratic elections.

1.3   Offences with which the accused have been charged are serious and were and still are prevalent.

15.   The parties further agree that a just and fair sentence, taking into account all the surrounding facts and circumstances will be as follows:

Count One – Each accused is sentenced 10 years' imprisonment
Count Two – Each accused is sentenced to 3 years' imprisonment
Count Three – Each accused is sentenced to 3 years' imprisonment
Count Four – Each accused is sentenced to 3 years' imprisonment
Count Five – Each accused is sentenced to 2 years' imprisonment
Count Six – Each accused it sentenced to 3 years' imprisonment.
Count Seven – Each accused is sentenced to 2 years' imprisonment.
Count Eight – Each accused is sentenced to 2 years' imprisonment

15.1   All the sentences in counts 1, 2 and 3 are to be suspended for a period of 5 years on condition that the accused are not convicted of murder, attempted murder and robbery involving violence committed during the period of suspension.

The sentences in counts 4,5,6,7 and 8 are also suspended for period [sic] of 5 years on condition that the accused are not convicted of possession of firearms, ammunition and any explosive device committed during the period of suspension.

16. The parties agree that the plea and sentence agreement are just and the accused should accordingly be convicted and sentenced as agreed.

Dated at Umtata on this 2 day of May 2006

APPENDIX E

Individuals Interviewed

Over a two year period, the team from the International Human Rights Clinic interviewed more than 50 individuals with a wide range of opinions and perspectives on the question of prosecuting apartheid-era crimes. In order to speak honestly, many interviewees requested anonymity. Those who agreed to be quoted by name in this document are listed below.

- Mary Burton, *Former TRC Commissioner, Activist*
- Madeleine Fullard, *Former TRC Researcher, National Prosecuting Authority Missing Persons Task Team*
- Ela Gandhi, *Peace Activist, Former Member of Parliament*
- Pumla Gobodo-Madikizela, *Former Member of the TRC Human Rights Violations Committee, Psychologist, Professor*
- John Kani, *Actor, Playwright*
- Paddy Kearney, *Former Head of the Diakonia Council of Churches, Consultant*
- Jody Kollapen, *Chair of the South African Human Rights Commission*
- Ilan Lax, *Former TRC Staffer, Attorney*
- Tshepo Madlingozi, *Legal/Advocacy Officer, Khulumani*
- Japhta Marawu, *Khulumani Member*
- Nomonde Mbangamganthi, *Khulumani Member*
- Mbuyi Mhlauli, *Applicant to the Constitutional Challenge to the Amended Prosecutions Policy, Cradock Four Widow*
- Brian Mphahlele, *Khulumani Member*
- Joanna Nkosi, *Historian, Consultant*
- Dumisa Ntsebeza, *Former TRC Commissioner, Advocate*
- Robin Palmer, *Professor of Law*
- Nyanisile Rohlihlahla, *Khulumani Member*
- Noluntu Sbukwana, *Khulumani Member*
- Jonathan Shapiro, *Political Cartoonist*
- Graeme Simpson, *Director of Thematic Programs at the International*

Center for Transitional Justice, Attorney
- Yasmin Sooka, *Former TRC Commissioner, Attorney, Executive Director of the Foundation for Human Rights*
- Dave Steward, *Executive Director of the de Klerk Foundation*
- Johanes Titus, *Khulumani Member*
- Jan Wagener, *Attorney to Adriaan Vlok*
- Leon Wessels, *Commissioner of the South African Human Rights Commission*

ACKNOWLEDGEMENTS

An earlier version of this book, released as a report in June 2008, was researched and drafted by students enrolled at the International Human Rights Clinic of the Human Rights Program at Harvard Law School under the direction of Clinical Director and Lecturer on Law Tyler Giannini and Clinical Litigation and Writing Fellow Susan Farbstein. The project was originally borne from discussions between Human Rights Program Fellow Rashida Manjoo and clinical student Zina Miller (J.D. '07) in conjunction with IJR Executive Director Fanie du Toit and Former IJR Executive Director Charles Villa-Vicencio. Clinical students Samantha Bent (J.D. '08) and Miles Jackson (L.L.M. '07) served as primary drafters of the earlier report.

Interviews and field research in South Africa were conducted by Bent, Farbstein, Giannini, Jackson, Miller, Clinical Advocacy Fellow Adrienne Fricke, Laura Dauban (LL.M. '07), Michelle Kim Hall (J.D. '07), and Amelia Thorpe (LL.M. '07). Villa-Vicencio and du Toit provided considerable guidance during that process. Student researchers, editors, and contributors provide invaluable assistance: Matthew Bugher (J.D. '10), Matt Carpenter-Dennis (J.D. '10), Tom Davies (J.D. '09), Kim Everitt (J.D. '08), Stephanie Finn (J.D. '10), Noga Firstenberg (J.D. '10), Katherine Glenn (J.D. '09), Morgan Hill (J.D. '10), Kavitha Joseph (J.D. '09), Zara Lockshin (J.D. '11), Katherine Simon (LL.M. '07), Esti Tambay (J.D. '10), Leigh Ann Webster (J.D. '10), Charline Yim (J.D. '11), and X. Kevin Zhao (J.D. '10). Fricke and Clinical Litigation and Writing Fellow Nate Ela also served in a supervisory capacity on the earlier draft. Communications Director Michael Jones designed the layout of the publication.

Our efforts would not have been possible without the support of those who advised and encouraged us. Their consistent and constructive engagement with our perceptions and analyses proved essential. The list of those due recognition is long and includes Ann Ashton, Jocelyn Bramble, Heather Capell, Dee and Rodney Coe, Ellen, Matthew, and Joe Davies, Judith Head, Robyn Hemmens, Todd Howland, Maureen and Rob Jackson, Ferentz Lafargue, Lloyd Lotz, Briony MacPhee, Richard Moultrie, Nothile Ndlovu, Joanna and Morley Nkosi, Thenjiwe Nkosi, Joel Pollak, Jeremy Sarkin, Natacha Thuys, Nahla Valji, and Howard Varney.

Finally, we are deeply grateful to the interviewees who enlightened us about these difficult and emotional issues. They graciously received us and openly entertained our challenging questions. This publication would not have been possible without the valuable insights they shared. Their fundamental generosity is evidence that the concept of *ubuntu* to which so many referred is not only an ideal or a wish, but also a reality.